THE RUNNER

THE RUNNER
Energy and Endurance

by Eric Newsholme & Tony Leech

Preface by Sir Roger Bannister, M.D.

FITNESS BOOKS
PUBLISHED BY WALTER L. MEAGHER

P. O. Box 382 Roosevelt, New Jersey 08555
21 Pitts Road, Headington, Oxford, England

THE RUNNER

Copyright © 1983 by Eric Newsholme and Tony Leech
Reprinted 1984
4th printing 1985

Design by Malcolm Grear

Logo by Wendy Gowling

Cover photo by Janeart, Ltd.

Composition by BI-COMP

Picture editing by Anne Feldman

Printed by Information Printing Ltd., Oxford, England.

ISBN 0 913115 00 2

CONTENTS

RC
220
R8
985

PREFACE

by Sir Roger Bannister, M.D.

It has always been my view that a knowledge of physiology and biochemistry makes exercise more interesting for a runner. The current running boom (for some almost an addiction, but if so the only healthy addiction I know) makes it necessary for the intelligent runner to know more about his body, how hard he should train, when he should yield to fatigue and what should be his diet and what are the limiting factors of his performance.

Dr Newsholme and Dr Leech are doubly fitted for this task—biochemists and teachers by profession and runners by personal choice. They bring scientific expertise and insight which ensures their book's success. Cannon's classical concept of the body's "wisdom" in integrating facets of performance is given fresh force.

At times I wondered if they verge on telling us too much. Can scientific knowledge destroy the simple pleasure of running barefoot on a beach with the wind in our face and the sound of breakers deafening us? Does the recreational runner want to know that the illegal and unethical blood doping may increase his performance by 5%, or that he would run faster if he decided to live at 7,000 feet but travelled to sea level to train, or if he took anabolic steroids? But science is not to be censored and we must take the new world of sport as we find it.

This book concentrates mainly, as befits the expertise of the authors, on the mechanisms of energy release which, rather than neural central drive or respiratory or cardiac function, now prove to be the more important limiting factor for runners. For sprinters it is a reduction of ATP, the "currency" of the cell, with lactate build-up and the release of protons. For marathon runners it is their dependence upon fatty acids as a result of declining stores of glycogen that makes them hit the metabolic "wall". By training based on long established but now scientifically verified principles of interval running, aided by dieting devices such as carbohydrate loading, the distance runners' capacity, however modest at first, may be dramatically improved.

It takes a lot of knowledge to write an easily read book. I am sure others will enjoy its style as much as I did, enlivened by some historical asides that take us from the over-specialized cheetah running at 70 m.p.h. and the versatile early man, a grazing animal and predator, now to 20th century man, recreator of an active style of life which can ensure a healthy, and just as important, a happier life.

Roger Bannister was the first person to run one mile in under four minutes.

1

THE BODY IN MOTION

Ability to move is without doubt the most striking characteristic of animals. The grazing animal moves to find vegetation; the predator to find its prey. Even if we stay in one place so many aspects of our lives depend on movement, such as speaking, urinating, breathing, eating, expelling a baby from the womb and playing a violin. All of these activities, and many more, are made possible because muscles can contract.

Muscles, as we shall discover, come in more than one variety but the kind with which this book is most concerned is skeletal muscle, which is under voluntary control and accounts for nearly half the body weight. During the marathon, these skeletal muscles consume about fifteen times more oxygen and fuel than the whole of the rest of the body.

Even more than most athletes, the runner demands the utmost from skeletal muscles and so is naturally interested in how they work, how they obtain their energy, what happens when they tire or are damaged and how they repair themselves. This knowledge also helps to explain why some people can sprint, some can run long distances and yet others are unable to jog a single mile. Aware of this knowledge, the runner will be better able to understand how training improves performance and how ageing eventually diminishes the performance of even Olympic champions.

Photo on left   George Hirsch, Bill Rodgers and Ellison Goodall

MUSCLES AND MACHINES

The internal combustion engine is a machine for converting the energy made available in a chemical reaction into movement. Since a muscle also does this we can expect similarities between the two. Indeed, both can give rise to linear motion and the overall chemical reaction occurring in each is very similar. But there are some important differences. In the engine, fuel combustion occurs in a limited number of places (the cylinders) while the rest of the engine contains this combustion and transforms some of the energy produced into movement. In muscle, the relationship between fuel combustion, energy production and the transformation of energy into movement is much more intimate and takes place within each muscle cell. A large muscle in the leg, for example the quadriceps, contains tens of thousands of these cells. Furthermore the fundamental unit which converts chemical energy into motion is just a small cluster of molecules of which a single muscle cell may contain millions.

Another difference between a muscle and an engine is the way in which the fuel is used. When the fuel reacts with oxygen in the internal combustion engine, a series of violent explosions occurs. These carefully controlled explosions release energy in the form of heat which expands the gases and so moves the pistons. In muscle there is no violent release of energy and although some heat is produced it is incidental. To achieve this conversion of chemical energy to movement, the chemical energy in sugar and fats is first used to make adenosine triphosphate, known by all biologists as ATP.

THE MECHANICS OF MOVEMENT

Of all the tissues in the body, muscle is the only one that can shorten. For such contraction to achieve useful movement each muscle must be attached at one end to something which remains fixed and at the other to something which can move. In man, like all vertebrates, the muscles are attached to bones which can move relative to one another if they are connected by movable joints.

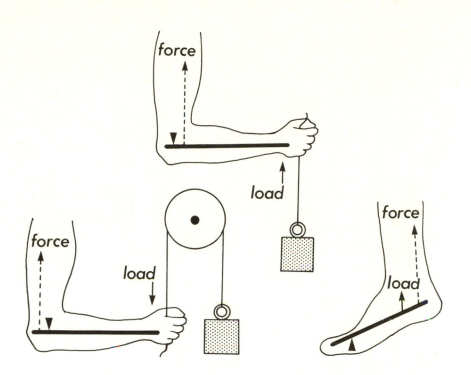

Diagram showing the arm and foot as a lever. The triangle (▲) indicates the position of the fulcrum.

The connections between muscle and bone involve immensely strong fibrous tendons.

In mechanical terms, muscle and bone form a lever. When a force acts on a rigid bar on one side of a fulcrum, a load can be moved on the other side of the fulcrum; this arrangement is known as a lever. In animals, the muscle generates the force, the fulcrum is the joint and the rigid bar is the bone.

Shortening a muscle provides the force to cause movement but this alone will not achieve locomotion; the process of shortening must be repeated in a cyclic fashion and for this to happen muscles must lengthen as well as shorten. But a muscle cannot, through its own activity, extend its length. When a muscle is not producing tension it is said to be relaxed and it is in this state that it can be

When the biceps contracts, the triceps extends, and vice versa.

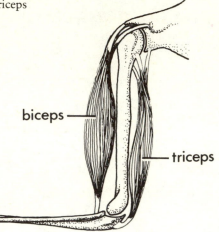

biceps

triceps

extended by some opposing force. In most cases this is provided by muscles on the opposite side of the joint pulling in the opposite direction. Such muscles are known as antagonistic muscles. In the upper arm, for example, the biceps pull out the triceps and the triceps pull out the biceps. But this arrangement depends on very fine coordination. A lack of coordination between antagonistic muscles could result in one tearing (or "pulling") the other. And even in the simplest movement many muscles are involved, each contracting or extending just the right amount at just the right time. Coordination between these muscles is essential to ensure smooth movement and pain-free running.

COORDINATION OF CONTRACTION BY THE NERVES

Electrical signals, carried by nerves in a series of impulses, coordinate muscle action. Each impulse passing along the nerve is a short-lived change in electrical potential (of about a tenth of one volt). In a single nerve, all impulses are identical. It is the differences in the intervals between the impulses which convey the message. But how does the frequency of impulses affect the muscle? If a muscle and its nerve are removed from an animal and stimulated artificially, the muscle continues to work, provided it is surrounded by a saline solution which mimics its normal environment. If the muscle is stimulated with a single impulse it responds with a single twitch, a shortening followed by a relaxation. The shortening takes about 0.1 second and relaxation 0.2 second. Some muscles are much slower, but the rectus muscles which move the eyeball have a twitch duration of as little as 0.0075 second. Single twitches are of too short a duration to be of any value in propelling large animals. But if a second shock is given before the muscle has had time to relax from the first, the muscle shortens again, and this shortening is added to the first, producing a more extensive and prolonged contraction in which greater tension is developed. If the frequency of stimuli is increased yet further, the muscle goes into a sustained contraction, termed a tetanus (not to be confused with the disease of the same name); but the contraction comes to an end when impulses stop arriving, and the muscle is then relaxed. Now, an increase in frequency of the impulses arriving at the antagonistic muscles causes them to contract, and this extends the relaxed muscle. The relaxed muscle can now generate a force by another contraction.

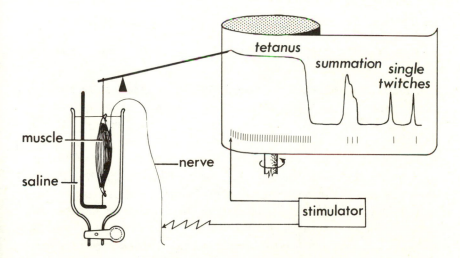

As the drum rotates, the tip of the lever scrapes a fine line of soot from the shiny paper on the drum, reproducing the movement of the muscle.

How a limb moves is determined not only by the nervous signals it receives but by its load. Load is the force opposing movement. To achieve a smooth movement, each muscle must send messages back to the brain, continuously informing the coordinating centers of the load, and of other changes such as its length and tension. The sensory receptors responsible for initiating such feedback are the proprioceptors, located within structures known as muscle spindles. These receptors are of the utmost importance in providing information for coordinating movement.

STRENGTH, SPEED AND ENDURANCE

Popeye's bulging muscles are the sign of his strength. This is reasonable enough since strength is proportional to the cross-sectional area of a muscle. Muscle strength is most important in sprinting, so that sprinters are usually large and have well-developed leg muscles. In contrast, the muscle of the endurance runner need not be capable of such a large power output but must maintain a constant power output for very long periods.

ATHLETIC ANIMALS

An indication of the immense power output of skeletal muscle and its versatility is gained from the feats of animals. Some migratory birds (for example the ruby throated hummingbird) fly 1,500 miles across the Gulf of Mexico in about 24 hours; the monarch butterfly can fly 2,000 miles at an average speed of 75 miles per day to reach its over-wintering site; and mature eels make the epic journey from the Sargasso Sea to the rivers of Europe—and back again—to spawn and die. Sprinters are also found in the animal world. A cheetah can accelerate to 45 miles per hour in 2 seconds and reach 70 miles per hour during the chase. Much greater acceleration occurs during the jump of a flea, which can propel itself a distance of 200 times its body length in a single jump. Compare this with the remarkable jump of R. Beaumont in the 1968 Olym-

pic Games in Mexico City (8.90 meters) which was only about five times his body length. Indeed all these athletic performances are superlative in comparison to the achievements of man but it must not be forgotten that man is an all-purpose animal. Individuals of this species have sprinted 100 meters in 9.9 seconds, run 26 miles 375 yards in 2 hours 8 minutes 13 seconds, covered 5,110 miles in less than 107 days (Max Telford ran from Anchorage, Alaska to Halifax, Nova Scotia in 1977), flown for one mile (with the aid of artificial wings but no additional power) and swum 21 miles (across the English Channel) in 7 hours 40 minutes. In addition, many of man's activities such as playing a musical instrument, typing a manuscript or striking a moving ball demand great precision of movement and an extraordinary coordination between the sensory and locomotory systems achieved by no other single species.

White and Red Muscle

Although the basic structure of all skeletal muscle is very similar, one visible difference does exist between the muscles of a sprinter and the muscles of an endurance athlete—their color. Since few opportunities for the direct examination of human muscles are likely to arise, these differences are more readily seen in the sprinters and endurance athletes of the animal world. For example, the pectoral (breast) muscle of a turkey or other game bird has a pale pinkish-brown color whereas that of a pigeon or duck is dark red. Game birds are flying-sprinters—they use their pectoral muscle only for escaping from predators or reaching a roosting place for the night. On the other hand, pigeons and ducks can fly many hundreds of miles nonstop. In fact, the two types of muscle are usually present in one animal, as in fish. If a grilled trout is laid on its side and the skin carefully removed, a thin line of red muscle (now brown after cooking) is visible and contrasts with the paler color of the bulk of the muscle. Despite its small proportion, this red muscle is the only muscle involved in normal cruising; the white muscle comes into operation only for more violent short-duration movements such as occur when a fish is caught on an angler's hook or a salmon is leaping rapids to reach a spawning ground upstream.

Human muscles also vary in this way. A sprinter's muscle will be whiter than that of the endurance athlete, although this difference may not be very striking. In fact, for most animals, including man, a clearcut distinction between red and white muscles cannot be made easily. All muscles contain both white and red fibers in a mosaic so that the overall color appears pink. More scientific methods of classifying individual muscle fibers have been developed which depend more directly on the molecular differences between them; these are described at the end of Chapter 3.

THREE KINDS OF MUSCLES

The kind of muscle referred to so far is skeletal muscle, which is also known as striated muscle because of the fine bands or cross-striations seen in the fibers under a microscope. The cross-striations result from the fact that the structural elements (sarcomeres) within the muscle are in register; such an organized structure is capable of a high power output. Skeletal muscles move our limbs, head and trunk and are used also in breathing. Since these movements are all under conscious control, skeletal muscles are also known as voluntary muscles.

A rather different kind of muscle is called smooth muscle because it lacks these cross-striations. Here the sarcomeres are less regularly organized within the muscle so that the power output is lower than that of skeletal muscle. Smooth muscles are responsible for some of the involuntary movements described in the introduction to this chapter—the movements about which we known very little unless they go wrong. Their tasks include squeezing food through the intestine, changing the diameter of the iris in response to variations in light intensity and controlling the flow of blood through small arteries. Smooth muscles are also important in activities over which we can exert some control, for example, emptying the bladder or expelling a baby from the uterus. Most of these movements do not require a higher power output; indeed if the muscles contracted too powerfully damage could be caused, but the movements must often be maintained for long periods.

The muscle of the heart is different from both skeletal and smooth muscle. It possesses properties characteristic of both the

At this speed, the Cheetah would complete the marathon with a PB of under 23 minutes. (Photo courtesy John Dominis/Life Magazine © 1977 Time, Inc.)

other muscles; the cross-striations are well-pronounced but contractions are not under conscious control. The power output is not as large as that generated by most skeletal muscle but it must be sufficient to pump the blood through all parts of the body. The rate of pumping must increase during running to supply the fuels and oxygen for the muscles. It must also pump non-stop throughout a lifetime which means contracting and relaxing approximately 2,500,000,000 times!

MUSCLES FOR RUNNING

The biology of man has been studied for more than a thousand years and tremendous advances in knowledge have been made in the last few decades. It is therefore surprising that so little is known about the mechanics of running. Precise details of the movements involved, the forces developed, the proportion of energy used for different purposes, which muscles contract and relax at any particular time and how these factors differ between various modes of running are still under study.

The main bones of the leg are the femur, extending from the hip to the knee joint, and the tibia, from the knee to the ankle joint. Two major muscles that extend along the length of the femur are the quadriceps femoris and the hamstring. The quadriceps femoris is in fact composed of four muscles that cover the front and sides of the femur: the rectus femoris, vastus lateralis, vastus medialis and vastus intermedius. At the back of the femur is a group of three muscles known collectively as the hamstring which comprises the biceps femoris, semitendinosus and semimembranosus. From the principles discussed earlier it can easily be seen that these two groups of muscles play an important role in knee extension and knee flexion. The hamstring is antagonistic to the powerful quadriceps femoris muscle and because of the enormous power output of the latter during sprinting, the hamstring is easily torn or "pulled". Movement at the hip involves at least two muscles, the iliopsoas and the gluteus maximus, with the latter forming most of what is usually known as the buttocks.

The two largest muscles in the lower part of the leg, the soleus and gastrocnemius, are situated at the back of the tibia. Together they are known as the calf muscle and their contraction extends the ankle. Much smaller muscles occur at the front and side of the tibia since their role in flexing the ankle is greatly assisted by the weight of the body.

THE ORGANIZATION OF MUSCLE

Just as it is possible to drive an automobile for a life-time without being able to distinguish a distributor from a differential, so an athlete can run well despite ignorance of muscle structure and function. For many, however, it makes sense (and is a source of pleasure) to have a working kowledge of their own machinery on which so much depends. As with the automobile analogy, knowl-

Major muscles in the right leg.

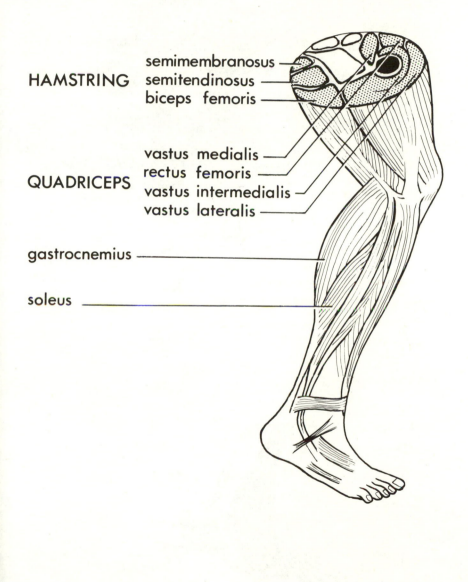

HAMSTRING semimembranosus
semitendinosus
biceps femoris

QUADRICEPS vastus medialis
rectus femoris
vastus intermedialis
vastus lateralis

gastrocnemius

soleus

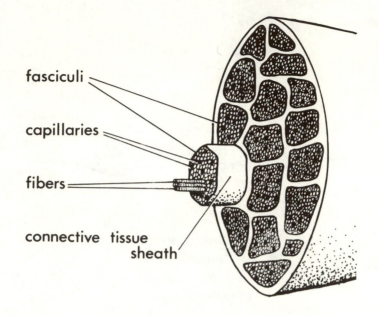

fasciculi

capillaries

fibers

connective tissue
sheath

The arrangement of fibers and blood capillaries can be seen in this cut-away view of a whole muscle. Intensive aerobic training can almost double the number of capillaries in a muscle, so improving the supply of fuels and oxygen.

Major tendons in the foot.

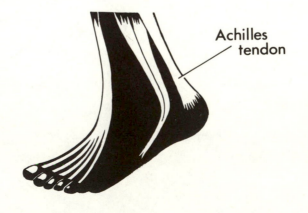

Achilles
tendon

edge is often gained as a result of a breakdown; the runner who has damaged a hamstring muscle will be acutely aware both of the location of that muscle and its function.

In any tissue, the fundamental unit is the cell and because in skeletal muscle these are long, narrow and cylindrical they are known as fibers. They vary in length from about one to 60 millimeters and in thickness from 10 to 100 micrometers (or 0.01 to 0.1 millimeters). For comparison it may help to know that a human hair is about 50 micrometers thick.

Each muscle is composed of many fibers. These are packaged into bundles of about one thousand, forming the fasciculi. Each fasciculus is surrounded by an envelope of connective tissue. Finally, each fiber is directly attached to this connective tissue, which also serves to link the fasciculi within the muscle. Hence muscle is composed of a number of partly overlapping packages of fibers extending throughout its length. The connective tissue contributes considerably to the strength and toughness of a muscle, as demonstrated by each mouthful of fillet mignon, a muscle that possess little connective tissue and so is very tender.

Not only does connective tissue surround and link the fasciculi but it also encapsulates the entire muscle as a sheath, separating each muscle from all others. At the end of the muscle this connective tissue, together with that within the muscle, increases in quantity and eventually forms the tendon which attaches the muscle to the bones. Some tendons are short, while others, such as the Achilles tendon, which attaches the muscles of the calf to the heel bone, are long.

ANATOMY OF A MUSCLE FIBER

Beginning at the outside, the fiber is completely enclosed in a cell membrane known as the sarcolemma. This is a thin structure approximately 8 nanometers thick. A nanometer is 0.000000001 of a meter. Composed of protein and lipid, the sarcolemma provides a barrier between the cell contents and materials outside the cell. Within the fiber, the most prominent features are the myofibrils, rod-like structures that occupy 60–70% of the total volume. It is

This electron micrograph of a toad muscle fiber shows myofibrils and other structures within the cell.

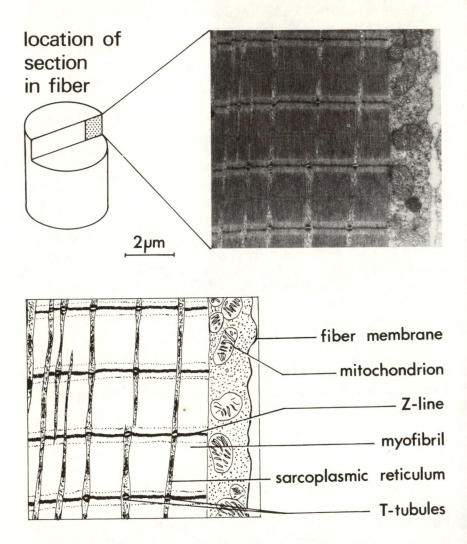

location of
section
in fiber

2μm

fiber membrane
mitochondrion
Z-line
myofibril
sarcoplasmic reticulum
T-tubules

these myofibrils which actually shorten and so are responsible for the contraction of the fiber.

Between the myofibrils there is a complex internal membrane system, known as the sarcoplasmic reticulum. This effectively isolates part of the space within the fiber from the myofibrils themselves. Within this reticulum space the concentration of calcium ions is about 10,000 times greater than in the rest of the fiber. A difference of this magnitude must be significant, and it turns out that calcium ions act as messengers within the fiber, linking nerve impulses with the process of contraction.

Outside the sarcoplasmic reticulum, but still between the myofibrils, lie the mitochondria. Each mitochondrion consists of two membranes. The outer membrane is a protective envelope, whereas the inner membrane is folded upon itself, filling most of the available space, and so providing an extensive surface within a small volume. Within the mitochondria, and especially within the inner membrane, occurs the oxidation of fuels and the generation of ATP. For this reason mitochondria are sometimes known as the "power-houses" of the cell. This description can be somewhat misleading since anaerobic muscles generate ATP without possessing any mitochondria. Mitochondrial ATP generation is, however, of primary importance for long-distance runners and the endurance-trained fiber contains many mitochondria each with dense foldings of the inner membrane.

Permeating the whole fiber, and between the mitochondria, is a material known as sarcoplasm. This is a whole kitchen cabinet of cellular chemicals, including ions, fuels, intermediates in biochemicals conversions, the enzymes catalyzing these conversions and the chemical building blocks for all the intracellular structures. Small molecules readily diffuse through the sarcoplasm, which links all the structures within the cell including its membrane.

Even this detailed account of fiber structure is not a sufficient basis for understanding how contraction and hence movement actually occurs. The journey towards this understanding is continued in Chapter 3 after consideration has been given to the important question of the muscles' source of energy.

2
ENERGY

A marathon runner is totally exhausted after running over 26 miles in maybe less than 2½ hours. A sprinter is exhausted after running 400 meters in about 45 seconds. Both athletes, it is said, have run out of energy. But is this really the case since other energy-demanding activities continue: the heart still contracts, the breathing muscles still function, the brain is still active and so are the kidneys, the liver and the intestine. The sprinter will recover quickly and within an hour or less after such a race will be able to perform as well. It will take days for the marathon runner to recover.

What then is the relationship between energy and endurance? We all know what is meant by endurance—the ability to run for long periods without becoming fatigued, but energy is difficult to define. One difficulty is that the term energy is used in an everyday sense ("I've no energy today") as well as in a precise scientific sense. If you ask a physicist what is meant by energy you will be told that it is the capacity for doing work, but we all have different ideas about what work involves! What is much more important than definition is the understanding that energy exists in different forms (light, heat, electrical, mechanical, chemical), that these forms are interconvertible, and when one form is converted into another there is no loss of energy. For the runner, what matters is understanding how chemical energy is harnessed in muscle, providing the mechanical energy required for movement.

Photo on left   Runners in the New York City marathon, 1978

ENERGY

A relatively easy way of measuring energy output is to run upstairs for a short period, just 4 to 5 seconds. If a number of minor factors are ignored, the gain in potential energy will be equal to the chemical energy expended. But we know that it takes more effort to climb stairs fast than to climb them slowly, so time enters into the equation. The amount of energy used in a given time is termed the power output.

Energy is measured in joules (abbreviated to J), a unit now replacing the calorie. One calorie is equal to 4.2 J. So to convert from calories to joules, multiply the number of calories by 4.2. One thousand joules are referred to as one kilojoule (kJ). Power output is expressed in watts with one watt equal to one joule per second and one kilowatt (kW) equal to one kilojoule per second. At rest, the power output of a human body is around 0.1 kW (about the same as an average light bulb). A non-elite marathon runner (3 hours best time) expends energy at about 0.8 kW but an elite marathon runner may achieve 1.3 kW. In contrast, a top-class sprinter can achieve a power output of around 3.5 kW.

Most of the energy expended in running appears as heat. But from where has the energy come? The answer is from chemical energy, and animals obtain all their chemical energy directly from food. Food is a complex mixture of chemical compounds, including carbohydrates, fats and proteins. All these contain chemical energy but this can only be released for use when a chemical reaction takes place. Burning is a chemical reaction in which the atoms

TABLE 2.1   EXPENDING ENERGY

Activity	Approximate Mean Energy Expenditure (kW)
Resting	0.07
Typing	0.10
Scrubbing floors	0.28
Walking	0.37
Squash playing	0.52
Carrying logs	0.85
Marathon running (elite runner)	1.30

within the food substance (for example glucose) and oxygen, the other reactant, become rearranged to form the products, carbon dioxide and water, which contain less chemical energy than the food. The difference in chemical energy is released and so can be used.

The energy content of our food can be calculated if we know its composition, since the energy released on burning one gram of carbohydrate is always the same. An average-sized meal contains about 4,000 kJ of energy and the average daily energy requirement is 13,400 kJ for a man and 9,600 kJ for a woman—the difference being largely due to body size. Since energy is released when food is burned, the amount of oxygen consumed is proportional to the energy released. It is useful for the runner to know that the consumption of one liter of oxygen will produce about 20 kJ of energy. Elite marathon runners consume about 4 liters of oxygen per minute, equivalent to about 80 kJ per minute; non-elite runners consume about 2½ liters per minute.

Chemical energy is a particularly useful form of energy because of the ease with which it can be stored (for example, as food in a freezer, oil in a storage tank or fat in the body). The food that we eat each day is stored in the body as chemical energy. In this stored form, which we call fuel, chemical energy is made available in a controlled manner during endurance running. Indeed, it is the *stored* chemical energy that provides the fuel for running, not the chemical energy immediately available from the food eaten just before a race. Running and digestion of food are mutually exclusive processes: they both place large strains on the physiology of the body. Although the nature of the food consumed in the build-up to a marathon is important, it should not be over-emphasized in comparison with the importance of the stored fuels and their mobilization during running.

THE ENERGY RESERVES OF THE ATHLETE

The body's expenditure of energy is continuous. Even while we sleep substances are being transported across membranes, macromolecules are being synthesized, impulses are passing along nerves and some muscles are active. But, in contrast, refuelling is intermittent; we eat only three or four times a day, so that the body must store energy for use between meals, or when a large amount of extra energy is needed, as an endurance running. Two storage fuels, each with a particular role to play in the economy of the body, are of especial importance—glycogen and fat.

Carbohydrate
Carbohydrate is stored in our bodies in the form of glycogen. It is well suited for energy storage, since each molecule consists of thousands of glucose units which can be released as required. As the glycogen molecule is extensively branched, simultaneous glucose release can take place at many points. Glycogen is a polymer of glucose. It is stored within muscle and liver cells together with the enzymes involved in its synthesis and breakdown.

Glycogen is not transported from cell to cell and must be broken down to glucose; glucose is the fuel which can be used by all tissues in the body. Surprisingly, the concentration of glucose in the blood is rather low but is maintained at a constant level. There is a biochemical control mechanism which ensures that when the blood glucose is used and the concentration falls, glycogen breakdown occurs in the liver, not in the muscle, replacing the glucose lost. The stores of glycogen in both the liver and muscle are replenished from the glucose absorbed from the intestine after eating a meal.

Why doesn't the body just keep all the glucose it absorbs in the bloodstream and so avoid converting it to glycogen, storing it, and then calling it out of store later? One problem is that glucose is a

TABLE 2.2   FUEL STORES IN THE AVERAGE MAN

FUEL STORES	FUEL RESERVES		HOW LONG DO THE RESERVES LAST? (MINUTES)	
	Gram	kJ	*Walking	*Marathon Running
Adipose tissue triglyceride	9,000	337,500	15,500	4,018
Liver glycogen	100	1,660	86	20
Muscle glycogen	350	5,800	288	71
Blood glucose	3	48	2	<1

*It is assumed that the energy expenditure during walking is about 22 kJ per minute and during marathon running (elite runner) is 84 kJ per minute. The amount of adipose tissue triglyceride will be much less in many elite marathon runners (perhaps 4,000 gram).

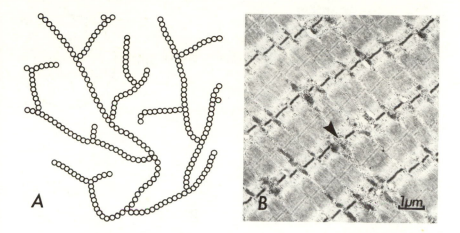

A) In this representation of part of a glycogen molecule, each circle represents a glucose unit. There may be as many as half a million such units in a single glycogen molecule. B) In this electron micrograph of part of a skeletal muscle fiber, glycogen particles can be seen as black specks between the myofibrils. A prominent group is arrowed. Each particle is a cluster of glycogen molecules together with the enzymes responsible for their synthesis and breakdown.

very reactive molecule and at high concentrations it can damage the proteins in the walls of the blood vessels so that they become thicker, thereby decreasing the rate of diffusion of oxygen and fuels from the blood into the cells. Glycogen, on the other hand is a much less chemically reactive molecule, and is therefore an ideal carbohydrate storage fuel.

Fat The other major storage fuel in humans is fat. Fat is composed of triglyceride molecules. Although the molecules are much smaller than glycogen, they are insoluble. This has the advantage that they are not chemically reactive and can be stored at a high concentration in the fat cell. Triglyceride molecules also differ from glycogen in containing proportionally less oxygen so their composition is closer to the hydrocarbon fuels used in internal combustion engines. Chemically, each triglyceride molecule consists of glycerol to which are attached three fatty acid units. Each part can be broken down to release energy but the fatty acids contain the largest proportion of chemical energy. In fact, several kinds of fatty

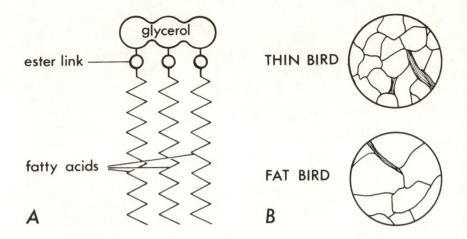

A) Representation of a triglyceride molecule based on chemical evidence. B) Fat cells from a thin wood thrush (after migration) compared with those from a fat wood thrush (before migration). Both are magnified to the same extent, showing that the number of fat cells remains constant while their volume, and hence fat content, varies.

acid occur in triglyceride, all having similar structures but differing in the number of carbon atoms (from 16 to 22).

Triglyceride molecules are stored in fat cells, which consist of about 90% triglyceride. The major function of these cells is to store the fat reserve and mobilize it when required. Fat cells form adipose tissue (body fat) but, unlike most other tissues, this does not form a discrete organ, and is widely distributed throughout the body. Beneath the skin (subcutaneous adipose tissue) it serves not only as a fuel store but also as insulation against heat loss; and around major organs, such as the heart and kidneys, it provides some mechanical protection. In men, the mass of adipose tissue at the front of the abdominal cavity (known as omental fat) can be embarrassingly large. In women, who can possess twice as much adipose tissue as men, its distribution is different, with more present in the breasts, the upper thighs and the buttocks, giving the more rounded form characteristic of the female.

The amount of adipose tissue in an individual body can vary greatly within a single lifetime. This is possible because fat cells can expand up to ten times in diameter, accommodating larger stores of triglyceride. Being able to add adipose tissue to the body is a key to survival in the animal world, providing energy during periods of enforced starvation (for example in hibernating bears) or for prolonged high levels of activity (for example birds on a migratory flight). On the other hand, it can lead to excess storage of fat which is not used—a condition known as obesity.

FUELS: MAKING THE RESERVES AVAILABLE

After many good meals and plenty of rest the energy reserves are safely stored away, triglyceride in adipose tissue and glycogen in liver and muscle. But now we wish to run a marathon and both reserves must be tapped to provide the fuels to enable us to run the 26¼ miles. The fuels are made available in two operations. First, the triglyceride and glycogen molecules are split chemically to form the fuels which can leave the cell. Then, except in the case of glycogen stored within the muscle fiber, the fuels are transported via the bloodstream to the muscles.

Both the storage compounds are split by a process known as hydrolysis, that is by reacting with water to produce their respective fuels, and fatty acids glucose. Glycogen is hydrolyzed in a reaction that is catalyzed by the enzyme phosphorylase to produce glucose 1-phosphate. When muscle glycogen is hydrolyzed, the

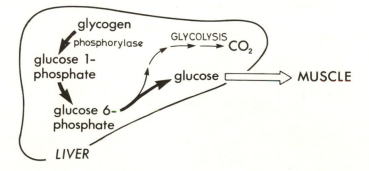

Making liver glycogen available as glucose for muscle.

glucose 1-phosphate enters the sequence of energy-yielding reactions without being converted to glucose; but in the liver, where glucose must leave the cell for transport in the blood, the glucose 1-phosphate is converted to glucose.

With triglyceride the hydrolysis appears simpler but the transport presents greater difficulties. The enzyme triglyceride lipase catalyzes the hydrolysis of triglyceride to produce fatty acids. These readily diffuse across the fat cell membrane but they are not very soluble in the blood, so that large quantities can only be transported by combination with a soluble protein present in the blood plasma, known as albumin. This protein combines tightly with the fatty acid molecules as they are released by the fat cell and transports them to the muscle. Although the binding is tight, the complex comes apart in the blood during passage through working muscles. This is because of the very low concentration of fatty acids that are free in solution due to their continual oxidation by the muscle. This transport mechanism is very effective but a price must be paid. The price is a limitation in the rate of fatty acid oxidation by muscle. The rate is limited by the low concentration of fatty acids that are free in solution. This is of great importance to the marathon runner. In essence, the limitation on the rate of fatty acid oxidation is responsible for the pain and fatigue in the final six miles of the marathon.

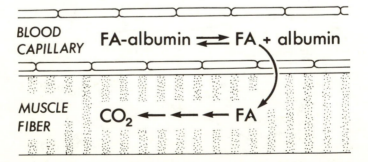

The oxidation of fatty acids in muscle fibers keeps their concentration low. In turn, this favors their diffusion from capillaries into fibers.

In summary, liver glycogen is mobilized as glucose, adipose tissue triglyceride is mobilized as fatty acids and both glucose and fatty acids are transported to muscle by the blood. In addition, muscle glycogen is made available as glucose 1-phosphate which enters directly the energy-producing pathway of carbohydrate metabolism in this tissue.

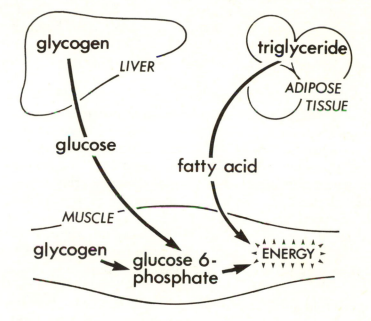

Three fuels are potentially available to muscle. Of these, liver glycogen is in relatively short supply and needed for tissues other than muscle. Reserves of triglyceride in adipose tissue are much larger but the rate at which fatty acids can be transported to the muscles is limited. On the other hand, muscle glycogen is readily available but inadequate to supply all the energy needed for a marathon. In the fuel economy of the runner, there is an optimum value in combining all three fuels.

CARBOHYDRATE VERSUS FAT

The amounts of stored glycogen and triglyceride are far from equal as can be seen from Table 2.2. In fact, 98% of the total energy reserves are held in the form of triglyceride, enough to tide the average man over several weeks of starvation. Why should this be? Fat is a far more efficient fuel for storage. For an animal that moves in its environment, the ratio of energy content to mass in a storage fuel is of paramount importance. This ratio can be compared for each of the two fuels by burning known amounts in such a way that all the available energy is released as heat which is then measured. The fuels undergo the same overall chemical reaction (and therefore produce the same amount of energy) in the laboratory as they would if oxidized in a cell. Burning one gram(g) of pure glycogen releases 16 kJ, whereas burning one gram(g) of a typical triglyceride releases 35 kJ.

This clearly establishes triglyceride as the more efficient storage fuel but the difference becomes even more pronounced when it is appreciated that in the cell triglyceride is stored in a pure state but glycogen is not. Glycogen is stored in association with a large number of water molecules. More than half of the mass of the stored glycogen is composed of trapped water so that triglyceride emerges as the better storage fuel by a factor of at least five.

If triglyceride is so efficient, why is glycogen stored at all? There are at least two reasons. First, the brain requires a constant supply of glucose, since it cannot oxidize fatty acids and the latter cannot be converted to glucose. Secondly, some cells cannot use oxygen and others occasionally need to generate ATP when oxygen is not available. Glucose and glycogen can be broken down to generate some ATP without involving oxygen—the process is known as anaerobic glycolysis. In contrast, fat cannot be utilized in the absence of oxygen.

ATP: BIOLOGICAL ENERGY

To an engineer, a machine is any device that transforms one form of energy into another. A muscle and an internal combustion engine are both machines which convert chemical energy into mechanical energy. In the engine, heat is a necessary intermediate, released when the hydrocarbon fuel reacts with oxygen. In the muscle, chemical energy is used directly to produce movement, with heat produced only incidentally. Remarkably, this vital process is identical in all muscles. From the flight muscle of an aphid to the hamstring of man, the reaction that releases the energy is the hydrolysis of ATP. In this reaction, ATP reacts with water to split off a phosphate ion, leaving ADP (adenosine diphosphate). Although the hydrolysis of a single molecule of ATP releases only a little energy, at least 10^{20} (more than a billion billion) molecules of ATP are hydrolyzed with each stride in a sprint. From where does all this ATP come?

The ATP Cycle
With a simplicity that characterizes life processes, ATP is made from the ADP and phosphate which are the end products of the hydrolysis reaction that releases the energy. Thus ATP is converted to ADP and phosphate, and the latter are reconverted to ATP. A very simple process, except that the resynthesis of ATP requires energy. This energy is provided by the oxidation of glucose and fatty acids within the muscle. The operation of a number of metabolic pathways that produce ATP together with the simultaneous operation of reactions that utilize this ATP constitutes the ATP/ADP cycle. Through this cycle, the chemical energy in food is harnessed to produce ATP from ADP and phosphate, and the conversion of this ATP to ADP and phosphate releases the energy required for movement. The importance of this cycle in energy transformation in the living cell cannot be stressed too highly.

Although at first it may seem wasteful that the chemical energy in glucose is transferred to another chemical (ATP) prior to its use in muscle, somewhat paradoxically this is actually an economy measure since a smaller number of metabolic processes is required in energy transfer. Muscle is supplied with a variety of fuels and these have to be processed in the body in different ways. Energy therefore is made available in many different reactions. The cells transfer the available energy to a single compound, ATP. Put simply, no matter how varied the food, all the available energy is

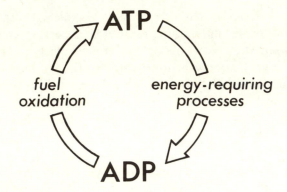

ATP links energy-producing processes to those that require energy. As both take place at the same rate, the concentration of ATP remains constant.

transferred to ATP. The economy now becomes clear, since only one reaction, the hydrolysis of ATP, is used to release energy from this end product of digestion. This economy becomes even more significant when it is appreciated that the hydrolysis of ATP drives *all* the energy-requiring processes that occur in the cell, from cell division and cell repair to the generation of electricity in the nervous system.

What ATP Does ATP can be described as the universal energy intermediate since it plays this role in all species of living organisms so far studied. But what is ATP? The answer might be "a nucleotide in which the base adenine is linked via the sugar ribose to a triphosphate group", or "a chemical compound that can be synthesized in a laboratory or purified from a living tissue which, when dried, appears as a white powder". But for anybody other than a life scientist what ATP *is* is unimportant—what it *does* is very much more important.

ATP fulfils a role in the cell analogous to currency in man's economy. No longer, in most communities, are services and goods bartered. They are exchanged for money. Money is then spent to obtain goods and services. In the same way, ATP is produced in energy-releasing reactions and used to drive energy-requiring processes. As with ATP, there is little point in asking what a dollar bill is—it is a thin piece of paper with hieroglyphics printed on it; it is much more important to understand what it can do. The great advantage of a currency, its flexibility, also applies to the ATP/ADP system. However, like all analogies, this one must not be taken too far; there is no counterpart in the cell to a bank where money can be deposited. ATP cannot be accumulated for use later. This is a problem because the amounts of ATP present in muscle fibers at any one time are small in relation to the demand for its use during exercise. For example, the concentration of ATP present at any moment in the fibers of the leg muscles of a sprinter is sufficient to power maximum sprinting for about one second; during the flight of a housefly, the ATP in the flight muscles would last only one tenth of a second.

The Constant Supply of ATP

What happens when a heavy demand is made on the utilization of ATP by, for example, running? Nature has solved this problem with an efficient control mechanism. The rate at which fuel is broken down is controlled so that it always meets exactly the demand for ATP. If you were to put down this book and run up some stairs, the rate at which your leg muscles would use ATP would increase several hundredfold. But so would the rate of fuel breakdown in the same cells, regenerating the ATP required. The mechanism of this remarkably precise control is described in Chapter 5. A feature of it is that it is the demand for energy and not the amount of fuel available which regulates the rate of fuel breakdown. If this were not so, the most obese people would make the best marathon runners!

There must come a point when ATP cannot be made fast enough to satisfy the demand. Suppose then that demand exceeds supply. The concentration of ATP in the cell would fall rapidly to zero, all energy-requiring processes would cease, and the cell would die. In muscle, the safety mechanism is known as fatigue and exhaustion. Fatigue guarantees that the power output is decreased to a level at which the rate of ATP utilization equals the rate of its generation. Exhaustion guarantees the survival of the organism.

TRANSFORMING FUEL INTO ATP

The ability of a muscle to work depends on it being able to use the chemical energy in fuels to bring about the synthesis of ATP. The reactions by which fuels are oxidized to generate ATP are conventionally divided into several metabolic pathways, including glycolysis, β-oxidation, Krebs cycle and electron transfer. These are all outlined in Fig. 2.7. Details of these processes are fully covered in biochemistry books, but what is important to mention here is the role of enzymes in metabolism. In metabolism each step, or reaction, can only take place because of the presence of an enzyme which catalyzes the reaction, that is, speeds it up so that it can play a useful part in the overall chemical change. Although an enzyme molecule can be used repeatedly for the same reaction, each kind of enzyme is able to catalyze only one kind of reaction. This means that a very large number of different enzymes must be present in each cell. Enzymes are very particular about their envi-

This diagram summarizes the metabolic pathways involved in cellular respiration. These pathways generate ATP using energy made available through the oxidation of fuels.

The central feature is a series of reactions known as oxidative phosphorylation in which ATP is made from ADP and phosphate, using energy provided by the electron transfer pathway. In this, reducing equivalents, denoted H, are oxidized by oxygen (O_2) to form water and at the same time regenerate the oxidizing agent needed for further fuel breakdown.

These reducing equivalents, mostly in the form of the molecule $NADH_2$, are produced as a result of triglyceride and carbohydrate breakdown. The pathways involved each consist of a series of reactions catalyzed by enzymes. The pathway of triglyceride breakdown, known as β-oxidation, results in the splitting of long fatty acid molecules into short acetate units. These become temporarily attached to a coenzyme A 'handle' to form acetyl-coenzyme A (AcCoA) which enters Krebs cycle. In this cyclic sequence of reactions, the acetate group is transferred to an acceptor and is oxidized to yield more reducing equivalents and to release carbon dioxide. The acceptor then picks up another acetate unit and process continues.

Through operation of the pathway known as glycolysis, carbohydrates (glucose and glycogen) are also broken down to produce acetyl-coenzyme A. As well as contributing reducing equivalents, this glycolysis also produces a little ATP directly. This is of vital importance under anaerobic conditions (see Chapter 5) when lack of oxygen precludes operation of the electron transfer pathway.

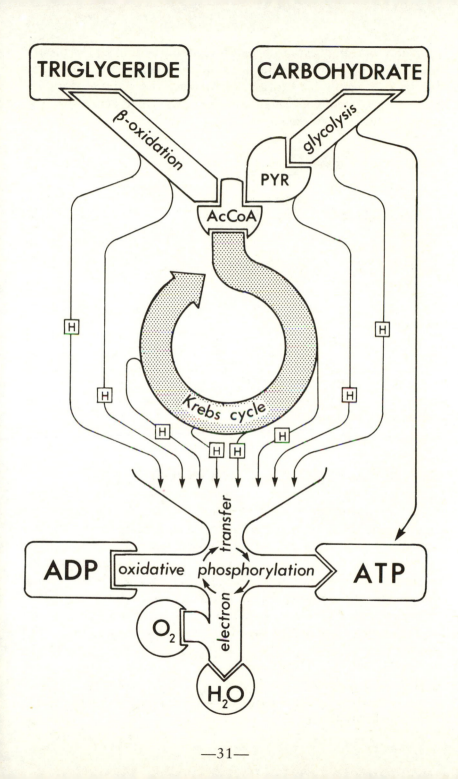

ronment, working best at normal body temperature and at precise concentrations of many chemicals in the cell. Changes in these factors can readily lead to loss of the catalytic activity of an enzyme with consequent decrease in the rate of ATP generation and possibly death of the cell.

TABLE 2.3   ATP TURNOVER

Tissue	Oxygen Consumption (Liters per Day)	Glucose Oxidation (Grams per Day)	ATP Turnover (kilograms per Day)
Brain	76	103	10.3
Heart	43	57	5.7
Kidneys	64	88	8.8
Liver	81	108	10.8
Skeletal muscle (at rest)	74	98	9.8
Skeletal muscle (marathon running)	5757	7710	771

Since the ATP yield from different fuels is known, it becomes possible to calculate the rate of ATP turnover in a tissue from its fuel and oxygen uptake, which are relatively easily measured. This is done here on the assumption that all the energy is provided by the oxidation of glucose although this is certainly not so in all instances. Note that at rest, the rate of energy utilization by the whole of the skeletal musculature is similar to that of other tissues, although on the basis of one gram of tissue the rate in muscle would be very much smaller. However, this rate increases dramatically in exercise and during a marathon race a runner consumes at least 500 liters of oxygen. This corresponds to about 700 grams of glucose, although in practice the marathon runner is more likely to use about 350 grams of glucose and 150 grams of triglyceride.

RUNNING: PENDULUM OR POGO-STICK?

From the heat produced and the oxygen taken up, we know that energy is used in running. Indeed we can calculate from either of these just how much energy is being consumed and even how many molecules of ATP must be hydrolyzed each second, minute or hour to provide the energy. But why is all this energy required? A stone dropped from a window of a tall building requires no energy to fall to the ground; a small push on an ice-rink will enable us to travel some distance without any obvious energy expenditure; 26¼ miles

Sir Hans Krebs, whose studies led to the concept of the cyclical series of reactions for the oxidation of fat and carbohydrate—the Krebs cycle, shown here on vacation in Bermuda.

can be cycled easily by relatively unfit individuals and walking is very much easier than running. But running *is* different from all these activities and requires a considerable expenditure of energy for at least three reasons.

As a runner moves forward, work must be done against the resistance of the air, known as drag. At a speed of 13 mph (just above the average speed of the elite marathon runner) about 8% of the total energy required for running is used to overcome drag. This will, of course, be increased by a head wind.

Unlike walking, running involves periods when both feet are off the ground—the floating phase. This enables the speed to be increased considerably above that of walking. But the floating phase can only be achieved by raising the center of mass of the body, which then falls to allow the next stride to be taken. You can see this, not with the unaided eye, but watching a slow motion film; the rise and fall of the body is then obvious, and this up and down movement costs fully 20% of the total energy expenditure in running.

The energy that is available in a moving object is known as kinetic energy, and in the runner can be subdivided into external and internal kinetic energy. Energy due to movement of the runner as a whole is known as the external kinetic energy; energy due to movement of parts of the runner relative to each other is known as internal kinetic energy. The two kinetic energy factors involve more than 70% of the energy required in running—40% for the external and 32% for the internal kinetic energy.

Whereas a wheel changes its point of support continuously and gradually while all the time bearing a weight, a leg only carries a load while it is on the ground and not moving. To move it must be free of a load. Hence running involves a cyclic alternation between a stationary loaded phase and a moving unloaded phase. This is not very cost effective in terms of energy usage. But it must not be forgotten that the movement of the legs and arms during running provides not only forward thrust and acceleration but also balance. We can therefore run not only on a flat road or track but on very uneven terrain totally unsuitable for a wheel.

Movement can be very efficient if kinetic energy is converted to potential energy and the potential energy then converted to kinetic energy. The best example is a swinging pendulum. At the top of the

The pendulum principle.

low potential energy
high kinetic energy

high potential energy
low kinetic energy

swing all the kinetic energy has been converted to potential energy whereas in the midpoint of the swing all the potential energy has been converted to kinetic energy. Hence the pendulum can move for a very long time with only a small input of energy to overcome resistance of the air and any friction of the bearings. To some extent this is what occurs in walking, so that energy expenditure is low. However, because of the alternation between loaded and un-loaded phases, it cannot happen in running. Unlike the pendulum, in running kinetic and potential energy rise and fall together so that one cannot be converted into another. The center of mass of the body is lowest (low potential energy) and is travelling most slowly (low kinetic energy) as the body passes over the supporting foot. As the position of the body rises and potential energy in-creases, acceleration occurs and hence kinetic energy increases. The increased energy expenditure required during running is the cost that must be paid for increased speed. An interesting project for an engineer would be to redesign man to enable "running" to be achieved as a pendulum motion—and calculate the best time for a marathon!

The kinetic and potential energy used in each stride is absorbed by the muscles and most of it is lost as heat. Indeed, to achieve locomotion all the chemical energy in the fuels is lost as heat—

The pogo-stick principle.

kinetic energy
in body
converted to
potential
energy in
spring

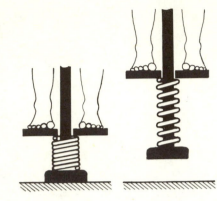

potential
energy in
spring
converted to
kinetic energy
in body

Of the five women running immediately before us, all are completely airborne
except the runner behind no. 6. Is this the pogo-stick principle?

hence the problem of elevated body temperature and heat stroke in marathon runners. Fortunately, not all the energy in each stride need be lost; some of the energy used in one stride can be stored and released again in the next. This is achieved by the presence in the body of springs—or at least structures that perform a similar function. Some of the kinetic energy is stored in the compression of the springs and released again in the recoil, during the next step. This is, in fact, the principle of the pogo-stick. Where are these springs located? The answer is in the tendons. They not only connect muscles to bone but since they have elastic properties they can act like the springs of the pogo-stick. Calculations indicate that the tendons in the legs, particularly the Achilles tendon, can store sufficient energy in each stride that the efficiency of converting chemical energy into mechanical energy increases from about 25% to 40%. In other words, energy storage by tendons reduces the overall energy expenditure by about 25%. The energy conservation may be even higher in elite runners and may explain what appears to the average runner to be quite remarkable athletic performances of Olympic champions. Unfortunately, this elasticity is lost with age so that less energy is conserved and consequently the pace is slower.

3

MUSCLES AT WORK

After watching an old steam locomotive get under way, a young child asked his father how the locomotive worked. It is very simple, he said, water is turned into steam and the steam goes into the wheels to make them go round. The child was not satisfied nor would the reader be satisfied if told at this point that ATP goes into the myofibrils and makes them shorter—although it does.

Running increases the heart rate and the breathing rate, and the runner can hear and feel these changes; but the greatly increased chemical activity in the fibers cannot be so readily observed. Yet, on this chemical activity performance depends. To use the automobile analogy again, it is as if we hear the fuel pump but not the engine. Of course the two are related and in the case of muscle this can be seen clearly only when we understand the way in which expenditure of chemical energy causes movement. In an attempt to do this, myofibrils and what they do for the runner are described in this chapter.

ARCHITECTURE OF THE MYOFIBRIL

Myofibrils are at the heart of the contractile process. When they contract the fiber contracts and when this contracts the muscle contracts. Although the chemical events within them cannot be

Photo on left   Alan Wells

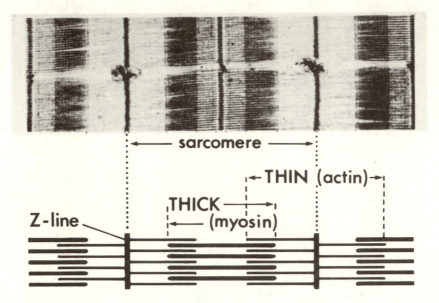

In this electron micrograph (of a frog sartorius muscle fiber) the myofibril can be seen to be divided transversely into units called sarcomeres. Each sarcomere, stretching from one Z-line to the next, is approximately 2.5 μm in length. Alignment of Z-lines in adjacent myofibrils (parts of two are shown here) accounts for the striated appearance of the whole fiber.

Projecting on each side of the Z-lines, parallel to the axis of the myofibril are the thin filaments. Lying between them, but not attached to the Z-line, are the thick filaments which bridge the gap between adjacent sets of thin filaments.

The filaments are made of protein; the thick filaments consist mainly of the protein myosin, where as the thin filaments consist mainly of the protein actin.

visualized directly, electron micrographs not only reveal intimate structural details, but also hint at plausible explanations of how contraction is actually brought about.

Within the myofibril, overlapping sets of protein filaments are organized into a regular array. When a muscle contracts the extent of the overlap between thick and thin filaments increases. This "sliding" of the thin filaments reduces the length of each myofibril so that the whole muscle shortens.

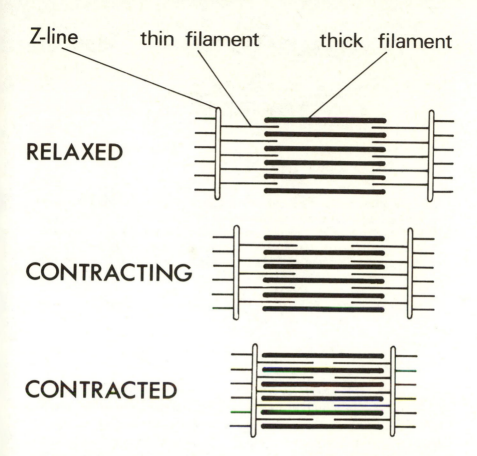

Z-line   thin filament   thick filament

RELAXED

CONTRACTING

CONTRACTED

Shortening of the fiber is a result of the thin filaments being pulled into the spaces between the thick filaments in each sarcomere of each myofibril. In most muscles, contraction is limited by collision between the thick filaments and Z-lines.

High resolution electron micrographs reveal that thick and thin filaments are linked by a large number of cross-bridges. These are not permanent structures but are able to break and reform over and over again. As they do, the cross-bridges bend so that they reattach further along the filament and in this way the thin filaments are pulled over the thick filaments. A rowing crew can provide an analogy for the process of contraction. The boat represents the thick filament, the oarsmen plus their oars represent the cross-

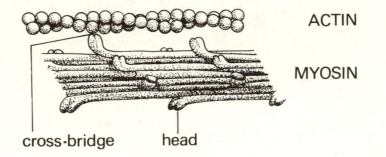

ACTIN

MYOSIN

cross-bridge   head

Each kind of filament is composed of a different protein; myosin in the thick filaments and actin in the thin filaments. Both actin and myosin molecules aggregate to form chains. In the case of actin, the individual molecules are more or less spherical but a large number of these combine together to produce a long chain, two of which wind around each other, rather like a rope, to produce the thin filament. The myosin molecule is a bit more complex and shaped somewhat like a golf club. To form the thick filament, the shafts aggregate to leave the heads protruding on all sides. These heads form the cross-bridges and are responsible for 'pulling' the thin filaments into the spaces between the thick filaments.

bridges and the water represents the thin filament. The oars are dipped into the water to make contact between the boat and the water and as the oarsmen change their visual shape, due to activity of a large number of muscles, the boat is moved relative to the water. The oars are then lifted from the water to repeat the stroke.

THE MECHANISM OF MOTION

At last we are in a position to relate all this structural detail to the knowledge gained from Chapter 2, that the ultimate energy source for contraction is ATP. The chemical energy in ATP can be released in a reaction with water, known as hydrolysis. The products of this reaction, ADP and phosphate ions, contain less chemical energy than do ATP and water, and if the reaction were carried out in a test-tube, this energy would be released as heat. Indeed if one gram of ATP were hydrolyzed in 15 ml of water (about four teaspoonsful), the temperature of the water would rise by approximately one degree centigrade. However, if ATP and water are mixed together

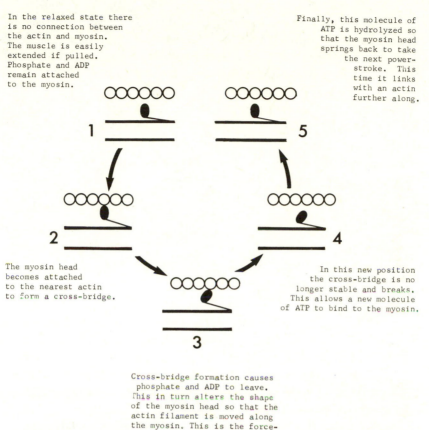

In the relaxed state there is no connection between the actin and myosin. The muscle is easily extended if pulled. Phosphate and ADP remain attached to the myosin.

1

Finally, this molecule of ATP is hydrolyzed so that the myosin head springs back to take the next power-stroke. This time it links with an actin further along.

5

2

4

The myosin head becomes attached to the nearest actin to form a cross-bridge.

In this new position the cross-bridge is no longer stable and breaks. This allows a new molecule of ATP to bind to the myosin.

3

Cross-bridge formation causes phosphate and ADP to leave. This in turn alters the shape of the myosin head so that the actin filament is moved along the myosin. This is the force-generating step.

A plausible hypothesis linking ATP hydrolysis with the cross-bridge cycle. The available evidence suggests that ATP hydrolysis does not occur during the power-stroke itself but is of course essential for completion of the cycle.

nothing actually happens. The ATP does not release its energy in any form. What is missing is a catalyst, something that will speed up the rate of the reaction without itself becoming changed in any way. In living organisms, all reactions are catalyzed by enzymes. Each enzyme catalyzes a different reaction so that many thousands of different enzymes are needed in organisms as complex as man and monkey.

The enzyme catalyzing the hydrolysis of ATP is known as adenosine triphosphatase, more conveniently as ATPase. If ATP, water and an ATPase are mixed together, the mixture becomes perceptibly warmer. However heat is not an intermediate form of energy in the process of contraction. The fact is that myosin (which forms the thick filament) is an ATPase that can catalyze the hydrolysis of ATP in such a way that the energy released changes the shape of the myosin molecule and hence the cross-bridge. This is what is needed to cause the filaments to slide over each other and so shorten the muscle. The myosin molecule as well as being a vital part of the structure of the myofibril is also the enzyme that makes it work.

WHERE ARE THE BRAKES?

One problem does remain. The cross-bridge ATPase and ATP are present in muscle at all times, even when we are resting or asleep. So why doesn't the enzyme cause contraction all the time and keep us awake? The answer is that the activity of the enzyme is strictly controlled. In fact, it will only work when there is a high concentration of calcium ions in the myofibril. Understanding how such a situation can come about involves taking a closer look at some of the other structures within the fiber. In particular, the sarcoplasmic reticulum, which is a series of membrane-surrounded sacs lying between the myofibrils. Within the sarcoplasmic reticulum the concentration of calcium ions is very high because they are being continually pumped there from the surrounding sarcoplasm by an ATP-powered pump. As a result, the concentration of calcium in the sarcoplasm and within the myofibrils is very low in resting muscle.

Whenever a nerve impulse arrives at a muscle fiber, calcium ions flood out of the sarcoplasmic reticulum and very quickly raise by about one thousand-fold the calcium ion concentration in the sarcoplasm and around the myofibrils. This increased calcium ion concentration causes changes in the filaments which unmask sites on the thin filament for interaction with the cross-bridge. Once these sites are unmasked, the cross-bridges attach themselves to the filament, ATP is hydrolyzed and so the cross-bridges bend,

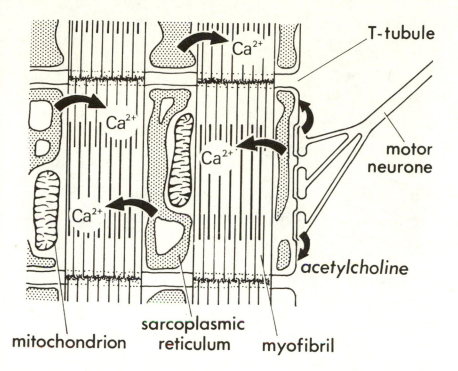

T-tubule

motor
neurone

Ca²⁺

acetylcholine

mitochondrion

sarcoplasmic
reticulum

myofibril

The control of contraction. When an electrical impulse arrives at the junction between a nerve fiber (neurone) and a muscle fiber, a small amount of a chemical (acetylcholine) known as the neurotransmitter is released. This triggers electrical changes in the cell membrane which are transmitted throughout the fiber via the T-tubules. This causes the sarcoplasmic reticulum to release calcium ions which initiate contraction of the myofibrils.

causing the thin filament to slide. The cross-bridge cycle continues with the hydrolysis of more ATP to ADP and the muscle contracts.

As soon as the nerve impulses cease, the process reverses. The leak of calcium ions from the sarcoplasmic reticulum stops and the pump, which has continued to operate, is once more effective in reducing the calcium ion concentration around the myofibrils. As before, the binding sites on the actin molecules are concealed from the myosin heads: if the oarsmen cannot put their oars in the water no force can be generated, and the boat does not move.

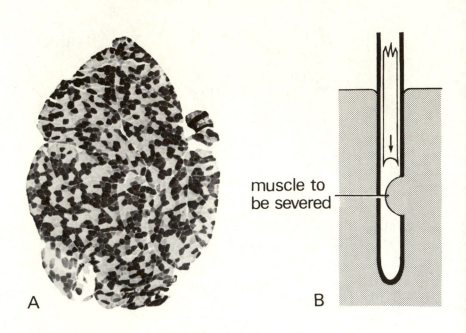

muscle to
be severed

A   B

A) This transverse section through a sample of human quadriceps muscle has been
stained to show fibers of different types. The staining depends on the properties of
the myosin ATPase they contain.

Very thin sections of the muscle are placed in a solution containing ATP which
becomes hydolyzed to release phosphate ions. These are then trapped within the
fiber by the addition of a soluble lead salt which reacts with the phosphate to form
lead phosphate which is insoluble. The next step is to make this lead phosphate,
which is white, more visible by converting it to black lead sulphide by treatment
with hydrogen sulphide gas.

This treatment would not distinguish fibers of different types were it not for
the fact that different pre-treatments can be used to inactivate the ATPase in
certain fibers. Such fibers do not stain and appear white in section. This section
has been treated with a solution at pH 10.3 to inactivate type I fibers and then
with a solution at pH 4.6 to inactivate type IIA fibers. As a result, only type IIB
fibers have stained. Although the biochemical basis of this differential sensitivity is
not known, it does provide a convenient experimental means of fiber typing. B)
The sample of muscle stained in (A) was taken from a human volunteer using a
biopsy needle of the type shown in (B). After insertion into the muscle, a small
sample is severed by depressing the plunger. It is claimed that even if several
samples are taken in this way, no more serious after-effects than slight stiffness are
experienced the next day.

DIFFERENT FIBERS FOR DIFFERENT TASKS

The basic mechanisms of ATP production and utilization apply to all muscles but, since not all do the same job, variation is to be expected. Some contract quickly, others slowly; some contract repeatedly, others occasionally; some have a good blood supply, others do not. Such variations explain the existence at the microscopic level of at least three different types of fiber in human skeletal muscles, namely types I, IIA and IIB. Most human muscles contain some of all three, although one may predominate, but in some animals there are muscles containing almost entirely one type. Muscles with a high proportion of type I fibers are known as red muscles and those with a high proportion of type IIB as white muscles. These differences in color reflect differences in the fuels used for ATP generation.

From the fatigue-resistant characteristics of red fibers it is not surprising that the muscles of good, and especially elite, long-distance runners have a high proportion of type I fibers. Many marathon runners have about 80% type I fibers in most of their leg muscles and it is reported that Alberto Salazar has over 90%. In contrast, many sprinters have a high proportion of type II fibers in their muscles and this is especially so for the 100 and probably 200 meter sprinter. Of course, even the correct fiber composition does not guarantee competitive success at the very highest level; training, commitment, temperament, encouragement and sheer luck all play a role. Nonetheless, fiber-typing and composition analysis are used by some coaches to select subjects at an early stage for training for particular athletic events.

4

THE MARATHON RUNNER

The marathon is an endurance event which is enormously popular in many parts of the world. In 1982 there were over 100 marathons in Britain and over 300 in the U.S.A. Why should this be so? The marathon has a mystique about it that may have something to do with its legendary origins but more probably because it provides a challenge of just the right level for widespread attainment. No one can say that running a marathon is easy but it is not impossibly difficult. To gain personal satisfaction there is no need to run the marathon well; simply to run it at all is sufficient—and then comes the desire to improve.

The marathon is run over 26 miles 385 yards (42.2 km) and is completed by elite runners in a little over two hours at an average speed of 11–12 miles per hour and a total energy expenditure of around 12,000 kJ. Although non-elite runners complete the distance in a longer time, their total fuel consumption is similar. The physiological stresses they endure may be even greater, however, because the elite runner is physiologically better adapted for running this distance. Indeed, the physiological stresses can become so severe that the runner has to give up. Hyperthermia (a catastrophic rise in body temperature), dehydration and even simple physical damage, such as blisters, can halt the runner. But the serious limitation for most runners is the supply of fuel. In this chapter, we see that exhaustion is not caused by the lack of fuel but by a change in the fuel mixture. The explanation of this limitation should make

Photo on left   Bill Rodgers

it possible to answer, eventually, whether the marathon would ever be run in under two hours, or whether a woman would ever run this distance faster than the fastest man.

HISTORY OF THE MARATHON

Pheidippides was an Athenian runner of the class known as hemerodromoi ("day runners") who provided a communication system between Greek cities and could cover distances greater than 100 miles in times similar to modern ultra-marathon runners. When in 490 B.C. the Persian invasion of Athens was imminent, Pheidippides was dispatched to Sparta, a distance of 140 miles, to request help from the Spartans. He completed the round trip of 300 miles in 3–4 days. The request was unsuccessful, but the Athenians defeated the Persian army at Marathon and Pheidippides may have been involved in the battle. He was then dispatched to Athens, a distance of over 24 miles, to inform the Athenians of victory and prevent them from surrendering to the Persian fleet. He is reported to have given the message and then fallen dead from his exertions.

In the ancient Olympics, such long distances were not raced; the longest race was probably over 3 miles (24 laps of the ancient stadium). In 1892, Baron Pierre de Coubertin proposed that the Olympic games be revived. This idea was favorably received and an international committee was set up to organize them in Athens in 1896. Baron de Coubertin was accompanied by Michel Bréal, a French linguist and historian, when he went to Athens to arrange the program for the Olympic Games. Bréal suggested a run from Marathon to Athens to commemorate the achievement of Pheidippides, and the Greeks, with their deep sense of history and pride, accepted it. The first race was run on April 10th, 1896 from Marathon to the Olympic Stadium in Athens, a distance of almost 25 miles and a Greek postal messenger, Spiridon Louis, won in 2 hours 58 minutes 50 seconds, probably equivalent to about 3 hours 10 minutes for the current distance. Of the 25 starters only nine finished, eight of whom were Greek, but its place in the modern Olympics was ensured. Races took place in the United

States soon after the first Olympic Games, in New York, on September 20th 1896, and in Boston on April 19th 1897, with the latter becoming an annual event from that time. Surprisingly, the distance was not precisely set and varied around 25 miles. In the London Olympics of 1908, the distance from the start at Windsor Castle to the Royal Box in White City Stadium was 26 miles but, at the request of Queen Alexandra, the start was moved back to the edge of the rough lawn so that the Royal Family could get a better view. The total distance was then 26 miles 385 yards. This was then fixed as the internationally accepted marathon distance in 1924.

RUNNING ON CARBOHYDRATE

Pasta parties and the popular press have made runners well-aware of the role of carbohydrate. Two carbohydrate fuels enter the pathway of glycolysis in a muscle fiber. First, glycogen, which is stored in the muscle, and secondly glucose, which is taken up from the blood flowing through the muscle. Since the quantity of glucose present in the bloodstream is very small, it cannot be considered as a store, but it is a fuel for muscle activity. To function as a fuel, glucose must enter the bloodstream, replacing the supply which has been used by the muscle. The glucose entering the bloodstream will come from the intestine, where it has been absorbed from ingested carbohydrate, or from the liver where it has been released by the breakdown of glycogen.

In assessing the contribution of carbohydrate fuels in the marathon it is necessary to know both how much carbohydrate would be needed if it provided the only fuel and also how much is actually used. This information is not easy to obtain directly; we have to use a little cunning. What we can do is to measure the rate of oxygen consumption during running, and for elite runners in the laboratory, under conditions that simulate the marathon, it is approximately four liters of oxygen per minute. This is equivalent to 5.4 grams of glucose per minute. In order to run the whole marathon on glucose, the elite runner would require at least 700 grams of carbohydrate. The non-elite runner would need just as

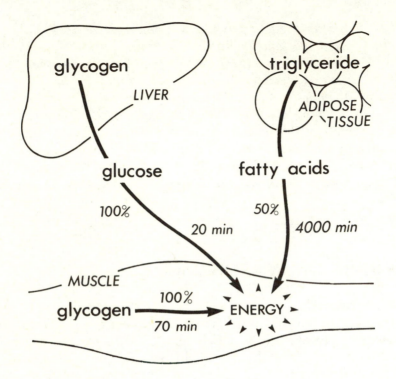

A summary of the three fuels that could be used during a marathon race. Against each is shown how long the fuel would last if it was the only fuel used during the race and the percentage contribution it *could* make to energy provision at any one time. It is clear that no one fuel can supply all the needs of the marathon runner.

much, if not more. We know that it is possible for a marathon runner to oxidize carbohydrate at this rate; theoretically, it could provide the sole fuel. In practice, this cannot occur since there is not enough carbohydrate stored in the body. The liver contains about 100 g and muscle about 350 g, a total of only 450 g, which could provide energy for an elite marathon runner for 90 minutes, at most. But even this is not possible, because some liver glycogen must be conserved to provide glucose for tissues totally dependent upon this fuel; for example the brain, which requires 5 g each hour. If blood glucose was used at a high rate for any significant length of time by muscle, it would lower the blood glucose concentration sufficiently to cause serious problems. Indeed, a decrease to

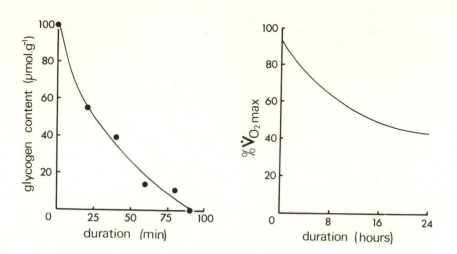

A) The depletion of muscle glycogen from the quadriceps muscle during strenuous exercise by trained volunteers on a bicycle ergometer. Samples were taken using a biopsy needle. Exhaustion occurred after 90 minutes. B) Average changes in the aerobic power output of ultramarathon runners during a 24 hour race. In the latter part of the race the only fuel remaining is triglyceride in the adipose tissue and power output falls to about 50% of maximum.

below 50% produces hypoglycemia in which the function of the brain is jeopardized.

These calculations tell us only that liver and muscle glycogen *could* contribute to the energy used in a marathon. To find out whether they do, the glycogen levels must be measured. It is not possible to obtain muscle or liver from marathon runners during a race! Fortunately, Scandinavian physiologists have used the needle biopsy technique to take samples from volunteers during sustained exercise on a bicycle. The studies showed that both liver and muscle glycogen is used during exercise of this kind and at a fairly steady rate over the whole exercise period.

Two important results arise from this work. First, it shows that exhaustion coincides with the glycogen stores reaching very low levels; and second, that the time it takes to reach exhaustion is directly proportional to the amount of glycogen in the muscles at the beginning of the exercise. The conclusion to be drawn from these two points is that the marathon is run on glycogen and when the stores are depleted the runner is exhausted, just as a car stops when it runs out of gasoline.

Although there is a great deal of truth in the conclusion drawn, we now know that the liver and muscle glycogen stores of the body are nowhere near sufficient to provide all the energy required to complete a marathon. How then is it possible to run a marathon? It can only be run if there is an extra fuel. The extra fuel is fatty acid.

RUNNING ON FAT

Compared with carbohydrate, the amount of fat stored in the average person is enormous. It constitutes about 12% of the mass of an average male and a much larger proportion of the mass of an average female (25%), although in many long-distance runners it may be as low as 5%. Because of its high energy content, the normal fat stores can supply at least the basic energy requirements for many weeks without further food intake. Indeed, if fat was the sole fuel, a calculation similar to that carried out for carbohydrate shows that about 300 g would be used during a race. On this basis, the average store of fat in man would provide energy for more than three days and three nights of continuous running. But if this is true, why does exhaustion occur so soon?

Before answering this question, we should first list the evidence for the view that fatty acids are used for endurance running.

- Adipose tissue triglyceride, when broken down, yields fatty acids and glycerol. Therefore, the concentration of these fuels in the blood indicates fat mobilization. Samples of blood, taken at various times during sustained exercise, show elevated concentrations of fatty acid, not only in man, but also in dogs and horses, both of which are good endurance athletes.

- By measuring the oxygen consumed and the carbon dioxide produced during running, the respiratory exchange ratio (carbon dioxide produced/oxygen consumed) can be calculated. For glucose or glycogen oxidation, the ratio would be 1.0 and for fatty acid oxidation 0.7. In fact, the ratio measured during endurance running is usually between 0.8 and 0.9, indicating that both glucose and fatty acids are being oxidized.

- Direct studies on the rates of utilization of blood glucose and fatty acids have been carried out by Drs. Philip Felig and John

TABLE 4.1   CONCENTRATIONS OF FUELS

| Animal | Time of Exercise (Minutes) | Concentration of Fuel in the Blood (mMolar) | |
		Glucose	Fatty Acid
Human	0	4.5	0.66
	40	4.6	0.78
	180	3.5	1.57
	240	3.1	1.83
Horse	0	4.4	0.29
	360	2.0	1.4
Dog	0	6.1	0.6
	60	5.5	1.1
	120	5.5	1.8
	180	5.0	1.9
	240	5.0	2.1

The values are means of at least six individuals. The humans (Stockholm firemen) were exercised on a cycle ergometer. The horses were ridden over 50 miles of hilly country at an average speed of about 8 mph. The dogs were run on a treadmill and the workload increased over the four hours.

Wahren on the firemen of Stockholm, who volunteered to be tested while riding a cycle ergometer. The tests confirm that both glucose and fatty acids are used throughout a 4-hour cycle, with fatty acids becoming more important in the later stages.

Exhaustion probably occurs long before all a runner's fat is consumed, because fatty acid oxidation alone cannot support the high rate of energy production required to run a marathon. Several lines of evidence indicate that fatty acid can provide only part of the energy demanded. If the carbohydrate stores are depleted before a run, so that fat is the only fuel remaining, exhaustion occurs very rapidly. This is an experiment you can readily perform on yourself. Obtain from a physician a diet that provides less than 25 g of carbohydrate each day but enough fat and protein. Follow the diet for three days and note your running performance. If you have managed to achieve this very small intake of carbohydrate, which is not easy, endurance will be much reduced.

In his study of ultra long-distance runners involved in a 24 hour race, Dr. Mervyn Davies found that after 10 to 12 hours of running the power output declines to a level at which the rate of oxygen consumption was about half of that achieved when it is maximum. After 10 to 12 hours, very little glycogen is present in the muscle or liver. Most of the energy must be derived from fat oxidation, and the running pace is only half of the maximal! In general, fatty acids are used during sustained running, but they can only supply about 50% of the energy needed to support sustained running at maximum speed. The difference is made up by oxidation of carbohydrate, mainly muscle glycogen.

Why can't the runner's dependence on fat exceed a paltry 50%? The problem seems to lie with the transport of fatty acids. Only a limited amount of albumin exists in blood to transport fatty acids, so that any rise in fatty acid concentration leads to the appearance of unbound fatty acids. These are most undesirable due to their tendency to disrupt membranes and so cause a number of unfortunate conditions described in Chapter 8.

USING A MIXTURE OF FUELS

The facts presented so far lead us to the view that the marathon runner should be using a mixture of fuels, fat and carbohydrate, for the whole of the race. At first sight this presents difficulties. Prior to the race the concentration of fatty acids in the bloodstream will be low since the athlete will be rested and will have eaten some hours before the start of the race. Furthermore, the runner will probably have been on a high carbohydrate diet prior to the race, so that most tissues will be using glucose. Even during the race the concentration of fatty acids, although it will rise, will not exceed that of glucose (see Table 4.1), so you might very reasonably think that glucose would be used in preference to fatty acids. But it isn't. When glucose and fatty acids are both available to the muscle, the fatty acids are oxidized in preference. Even more important to the runner, the control system ensures that as much fatty acid oxidation as possible takes place up to about 50% of the maximum oxygen uptake, but the remainder of the energy is generated by the oxidation of blood glucose or muscle glycogen. It is a mechanism that always allows a mixture of fuels to be used by the muscles. The advantage of this is that it "spares" carbohydrate so that the limited stores will last longer.

What control mechanism restricts oxidation of carbohydrate when fatty acids are being used? To answer this it is necessary to consider the metabolic pathway by which glucose or glycogen is oxidized.

Before glucose can enter the oxidative pathway in muscle it has to be converted to pyruvate in a process known as glycolysis. The rate of this process is determined by the concentration of ATP in the fiber. Above all else, a constant concentration of ATP is maintained despite changes in the rate of ATP utilization. This negative feedback control mechanism is especially important in sprinting so is further discussed in Chapter 5. In the present context, the important point is that fatty acid oxidation increases the effectiveness of ATP as a feedback inhibitor of glycolysis so that when fatty acids are oxidized by muscle, less glucose and glycogen are used.

As well as providing a scientific basis for evaluating the best food to consume before, during and after a marathon, a number of

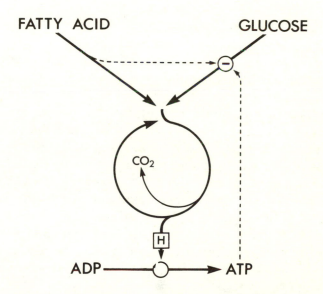

The rate at which ATP is made precisely matches the rate at which it is used. Its synthesis from glucose or glycogen is controlled by a negative feedback loop in which ATP inhibits glycolysis. ATP synthesis from fatty acids depends on the availability of ADP because electron transfer cannot take place unless oxidative phosphorylation occurs. The inhibition of glycolysis by fatty acid oxidation ensures that fatty acids are used in preference to glucose when both are available.

other consequences of this control mechanism are important to the runner. If the demand for energy by the muscle increases during a run, because for example the runner increases his speed, the ATP concentration will fall, and it is primarily the rate of carbohydrate utilization and not that of fat which will increase. This increased rate will be maintained until the energy demand is decreased or until the body runs out of carbohydrate and fatigue results. This underlines the importance of maintaining a steady pace.

The runner who runs more than about 10 miles in the morning before breakfast will use up all the glycogen in the liver during the run and must then rely upon fatty acid oxidation to prevent a high rate of glucose utilization by the muscle. If too much glucose were used, hypoglycemia, with the dangers of coma and death, would result. The effectiveness of this safety device is demonstrated by one of the authors who regularly runs 20 miles after 20 hours fasting without any signs of hypoglycemia.

FATIGUE

The reward for struggling through the section on control of fuel supply is now at hand—an understanding of the basis of fatigue and exhaustion in marathon running. Fatigue is defined as the inability to maintain power output. But the runner can define it more personally as discomfort followed by pain which eventually becomes so severe that the only escape is to stop running. There is no doubt that discomfort and pain are warning signs, telling us that energy expenditure is exceeding, or soon likely to exceed, the rate at which ATP can be generated. Damage to the muscle is forestalled by heeding the body's warning. On the other hand, many runners know that in training hard or racing to improve personal performance, not every sign of pain can be heeded. Experienced runners monitor their pain and take seriously the dangers that may lie ahead.

The intriguing question is what causes fatigue, and a number of possibilities have been suggested, all of which probably play some part. Loss of body fluid (dehydration) is one factor. It decreases blood volume and reduces the rate of supply of blood-borne fuels to the muscle. During running the body temperature

Walking to the finish line, London marathon.

increases and on a warm day this causes a massive diversion of blood to the skin for cooling, depriving the muscles of fuel and oxygen, and so precipitating exhaustion. These problems can be avoided by careful preparation before and vigilance during the race.

The most common cause of fatigue is almost certainly metabolic. Many runners experience severe fatigue between 18 and 24 miles; progress is painfully slow and accompanied by an overwhelming desire to stop running. This is known as "hitting the wall." With the information presented above it is possible to suggest a metabolic explanation of "the wall".

Explaining "The Wall"

Up to the 17th or 18th mile, the runner has probably been operating at about 80% of maximum aerobic capacity ($V_{O_2 max}$), oxidizing both fatty acids and glucose. The glycogen stores in the muscle now become depleted, and so the rate of carbohydrate oxidation decreases. Unfortunately, fatty acid oxidation cannot provide all the ATP required. Consequently, if the high power output is maintained, the ATP concentration must fall, for it is now being used faster than it can be generated. Here then is the cause of fatigue: the fall in ATP concentration in muscle. The pace slackens, and the pain increases. But what is the relationship between the fall in the ATP concentration, the slackening of pace and the pain?

The decrease in ATP concentration leads to a decrease in the contractile activity of the muscle. Probably this happens indirectly, by inhibition of the myosin ATPase of the cross-bridge, decreasing the rate of cross-bridge cycling and hence the power output. The pace slackens. It is sometimes suggested that exhaustion occurs when the ATP in the muscle runs out; this cannot be correct since ATP is required for other vital processes in the muscle. What is likely is that a safety mechanism exists in muscle which "senses" a decrease in the ATP concentration and automatically reduces the rate at which it is used.

The sensation of discomfort and pain is another symptom of fatigue. Although we don't know how this is brought about, it is possible that the decrease in ATP concentration causes the release of a chemical from the muscle fibers which stimulates sensory nerve endings within the muscle, sending impulses to the brain which are "interpreted" as discomfort or pain depending on their frequency. The greater the decrease in the ATP concentration in muscle, the greater would be the amount of the chemical released and hence the greater the frequency of sensory impulses to the brain.

In endurance races, almost all participants slow down as the race proceeds and the winner is usually the athlete who slows down least. In terms of fuel supply, the slowing down allows fatty acid oxidation to provide a greater proportion of the energy demand as the glycogen reserves become depleted. A hypothetical example should make this clear. A certain marathon runner can run a mile no faster than 6 minutes 20 seconds; we will take this as an indication of the runner's maximum aerobic power output. Suppose this runner's best time for the marathon is 3 hours 28 minutes, so that on average each mile is run in 8 minutes. Since power output is approximately proportional to speed, this means that the runner goes at 80% of the maximum power output for the whole marathon. Let us assume that, for most of the race, fatty acid and glucose oxidation contribute equally to the power output (that is, 40% of the maximum for each fuel) but that, at 22 miles, liver and muscle glycogen reserves run out. At this stage, the contribution from carbohydrate oxidation would be lost, so that the power output would fall from 80% to 40% of maximal and hence the runner's speed would fall from 8 minutes per mile to around 16 minutes per mile or less than 4 miles per hour. This explanation would account for the fact that many non-elite runners begin to walk in the later stages of the race despite every effort to keep running.

Elite marathon runners do not normally experience "the wall" probably because their muscles can remove fatty acids more effectively from the blood, so that their glycogen stores will last for the duration of the race. There is evidence that training does increase this ability and elite runners may be able to support as much as 70% of their maximum aerobic power output by fatty acid oxidation. The experienced runner will also have learned to consume energy at the optimum rate. If a race is finished with some glycogen remaining in the muscles a faster time would have been possible; if the reserve runs out before the end of the race, fatigue will occur, the pace will decrease and the time of completion will increase.

Gluconeogenesis
One means by which extra glucose could be produced under conditions of fatigue does deserve consideration. Some of the protein of the muscle may break down to provide amino acids which can be converted to glucose in the liver. The conversion of amino acids to glucose is known as gluconeogenesis, which simply means new glucose synthesis or glucose synthesized from non-carbohydrate sources. This yields an extra supply of glucose and could allow the runner to "penetrate the wall". However, the amount of glucose that could be provided in this way would be small, and achieved only at the expense of damage to the muscle. The earlier gluconeogenesis occurs in the race, the greater the muscle damage. Although there is no doubt that muscle protein breaks down both during and after a race, a large increase in the rate of breakdown during the race is undesirable.

Conclusion
The marathon is beyond the normal physiological limit of fuel supply for all except extremely well-trained runners.

The distance is too long and the pace is too fast. Metabolically, man is a long-distance walker, not a marathon runner. Only if fatty acid oxidation provided all the energy requirements could man run long distances easily.

MANAGING METABOLISM

Based on the information provided in the earlier part of this chapter, a number of practical suggestions can be made to overcome some of the problems of marathon running.

Glycogen Loading One tactic is to increase the amount of glycogen stored in the body. There are two ways to do this, the "unloading-loading" diet and the "loading" diet. In the former, muscle glycogen levels are decreased by an exhaustive run six days prior to the competition. The runner then eats a low carbohydrate diet for three days and once again runs to exhaustion to deplete muscle glycogen. Then for the final three days up to the competition the runner eats a high carbohydrate diet (the period on the high carbohydrate diet may be different for different runners, as discussed below). "Supercompensation" now occurs as more glycogen is synthesized than was used up by the exhaustive runs. This dietary regime increases the muscle glycogen level two-fold in some runners. It was probably first used by the British marathon runner, Ron Hill, in preparation for the 1969 European Championship in Athens; Hill won the marathon.

Although there is no doubt that many marathon runners believe that it is important to elevate their glycogen levels prior to a race, the need for the 3-day period on the low carbohydrate diet has been questioned. Since many marathon runners cover a very large mileage in training every week (100 miles or more) they probably deplete their glycogen stores every day so that during intensive training these stores are always below normal. A period on a low carbohydrate diet is therefore *not* necessary to maintain low carbohydrate stores. Indeed, for many athletes it decreases the duration of training runs, and it may increase susceptibility to viral infections. While marathon runners training less than about 50 miles per week should benefit from the "unloading-loading" diet,

THE OBSERVER, 28 SEPTEMBER 1969

CHRISTOPHER BRASHER finds the key to
Ron Hill's marathon success in the European Games in Athens last Sunday.

Licking them with honey

On Monday, when the sun is hot,
I wonder to myself a lot:
' Now is it true, or is it not . . .'
THOSE lines were written by
Pooh, who said of himself ' I
am a bear of Very Little Brain
. . .' which is, I think, overplay-
ing the false British modesty.
(He was a very British bear.)

After all, he was a bear who
lived on a very intelligent diet of
honey, which is just what marathon
runners should do on Sunday,
Saturday, Friday and Thursday if
they're going to win a gold medal
on Sunday. Which brings me to
the subject of diet.

There are some standard questions which every athlete is asked
when he returns home after a big
success. They start with: ' What
did you feel when you won ?'
And end, after a few pints of beer,
with a confidential leer: ' Tell me
. . . do you have to keep off sex ?'
I have often wondered, now that
women's athletics are so popular,
if the successful girls get asked
the same range of questions. But
I will guarantee that they will be
asked about diet, one of the obses-
sions of our age. It always struck
me as a rather tiresome question
with the implication that gimmicks,
instead of hard work, could win
major titles.

Not so any longer. Ron Hill
won last Sunday's marathon—from
Marathon itself to the old 1896
stadium in Athens—with the aid
of a diet.

Breakthrough ?

Now on Sunday, in the excitement of the moment, I might have
written an article saying that this,
at last, was the scientific breakthrough that his diet was all-
important. But on Monday when
the sun was hot in Athens I
wondered to myself a lot: ' Now
is it true or is it not ?' And the

Ron Hill—felt the benefit of the ' over-shooting phenomenon.'
ED LACEY

next three days. So you eat a high
protein/fat diet and train quite
hard.

A high protein/fat diet would
consist of something like this:—
Breakfast: A large plateful of eggs

After three or four days of this
diet, with little or no training, you
will have enough fuel stored up to
do what Ron Hill did to Gaston
Roelants in the last four to five
miles of the marathon.

The diet was discovered, about
three years ago, by a couple of
Swedish scientists called Bengt
Saltin and Lars Hermansen. They
showed that a person's capacity for
prolonged heavy exercise is limited
by his available stores of carbohydrate—which is basically the
glycogen content of his muscles. A
normal average value for this would
be about 1.5 per cent of glycogen
by weight.

By messing around with your
diet, it is possible to raise this percentage of glycogen. But for some
peculiar reason which is not yet
understood, the most effective pro-
cedure is to exhaust all the glycogen
in the muscles and then keep the
glycogen content low for a few
days by eating this fat and protein
diet.

Then, when you switch to a high
carbohydrate diet your glycogen
starved muscles go through what is
known as ' an over-shooting phenomenon '—so much so that the glycogen content of the muscles can become as high as 5 per cent.

Slow process

None of this will do the marathon
runner any good at the beginning
or in the middle of the race. Then
he has to rely on his fitness, speed
and stamina. But after about two
hours of really fierce exercise the
normal glycogen supplies become
exhausted and the runner has to
start burning fat for fuel—a slow
process.

So one explanation of what hap-
pened in the last few miles during
the Athens marathon is that Roelants had exhausted his glycogen
supplies and was burning fat, while
Hill was using the extra glycogen

degrees Fahr
denly felt goo
Last week I
of temperatu
plain Dick '1
10,000 metres
to task by an
says that I '
other explana
say that ' if
was indeed
Fahrenheit at
as Brasher st
have been :
acute infectiv
therefore, not
all.'

And the d
by challengir
performance
at 105 degre
he says, ' is
the case, sin
probably her
versible com
I'm sure th
mal patient,
not normal |
not undergoi
Griffith Pug
Research Co
some of his
athlete's tem;
as 106.3 deg
Johnston an
the normal
modern disti
to 50 minut
about 103 de
the normal l
formance s
sharply is
Fahrenheit.
So if Hill
his temperat
more as he
would never
bad patch. (
would have 1
as possible
No major
advanced in
and diet and
very effective

Ron Hill

those covering more miles than this, and probably depleting their
glycogen more frequently, would be better advised to follow the
"loading" diet.

On the "loading" diet a large quantity of carbohydrate is eaten
in the few days before the race, without the preliminary low carbohydrate period. Timing is crucial. The "extra" glycogen will
only persist in the muscles for a short time, even in the absence of
exercise. Most athletes using this technique consume the high carbohydrate diet two to four days before the event. Although pasta
parties the night before the race are popular, the benefit is largely
social. In most cases, it is probably too late for effective loading.

A number of clues provide some information about the progress of glycogen loading and help an individual get the amount and
timing right for his or her body. First, if too much carbohydrate is
ingested, diarrhea occurs, because unabsorbed sugars pass into the
large intestine where they interfere with water uptake. Secondly,
the increased glycogen content of the body can be monitored by

careful weighing at the same time each morning since a full "load" of glycogen plus associated water can weigh about two pounds. Finally, unloading is accompanied by an abnormally high rate of urine production because of all the water trapped in association with glycogen stores. If this occurs before the race, loading was begun too early.

In what form should extra carbohydrate be taken? The normal response of the body to food is to replenish glycogen stores first and then to convert any additional carbohydrate to fat for storage in adipose tissue. The marathon runner needs to encourage the former but discourage the latter. This can be done by eating normal amounts of food at each meal but eating more meals and increasing the proportion of carbohydrate. The best pattern is three or four normal meals spaced out over the day with a couple of small meals (snacks) in between. The nature of the carbohydrate is also important. It should be complex carbohydrate, not simple sugars, so that bread, potatoes, cereals, rice, pearl barley and pasta are beneficial.

Complex carbohydrates are digested slowly so that absorption of sugar into the body takes place over a long time and this encourages the storage of glycogen instead of fat. The intake of food containing the simple sugars, such as chocolate bars, sweetened drinks, honey and jam should not be excessive and only accompany the complex carbohydrate. The rate of digestion depends not only on the state of the carbohydrate but also on the presence of fat and protein, which slow down the rate at which foods pass through the small intestine and therefore favor the slow absorption of glucose. For this reason, meat, cheese, fish or egg should be eaten at each main meal but in smaller quantities than usual, since carbohydrate must replace some of the protein. An important point is that, since glycogen is stored in association with water, the intake of fluid has to be increased during the "loading" phase. Runners should be able to monitor this by observing the color of their urine; when insufficient fluid is being taken the urine becomes more amber.

On the day preceding the race some runners find it beneficial to eat little or nothing after the evening meal. But the intake of fluid should be maintained. If the runner is well-rested, then very little glycogen will be used during this period of starvation, which should then encourage the release of fatty acids from adipose tissue depots. Not everyone will want to choose this strategy, and many runners find they run better after a good carbohydrate breakfast. But, for reasons given below, the breakfast should be taken several hours before the race.

Sometimes after glycogen loading the legs feel "heavy" during the first few miles of the race. If this is due to the weight of the extra glycogen plus water in the muscles, the feeling should disappear as the fuel is used; but if the "heavy" feeling persists, and particularly if it becomes worse, the runner should consider dropping out of the run, for this may be a sign of the early stages of a viral attack. Virus infection may impair control mechanisms, lead to very high levels of fatty acids, and so increase the risk of a heart attack.

Glucose Before the Race?

If the amount of carbohydrate stored by the body limits the marathon runner, does it not make metabolic sense to eat easily-digested carbohydrate, such as glucose or chocolate bars, just before the race? The answer is *no* and the reason is rather interesting. The mobilization of fatty acids during endurance running is largely due to changes in the blood levels of two important hormones, epinephrine and insulin. Epinephrine stimulates fatty acid mobilization, insulin inhibits it.

Epinephrine is released by the adrenal gland in response to excitement and stress immediately before the race and its release increases further during the race. The insulin level decreases as the race proceeds, and these changes together probably account for the smooth increase in the rate of mobilization of fatty acids during a run. However, eating glucose, or foods containing carbohydrate, causes the release of large amounts of insulin into the bloodstream, inhibiting fatty acid mobilization just when it is needed to conserve valuable glycogen stores. This emphasizes the integrated nature of metabolic processes in the body.

Glucose During the Race?

If it's no to chocolate before the race, how about during the race? The answer is a qualified yes. After about 15 miles of running, easily digested carbohydrate can be taken. At this stage, it does not result in insulin secretion. (The secretion may be prevented by the high concentration of epineph-

The mobilization of fatty acids from triglyceride in adipose tissue is regulated by a number of chemical factors. Conditions which favor the release of fatty acids are likely to enhance the marathon runner's performance.

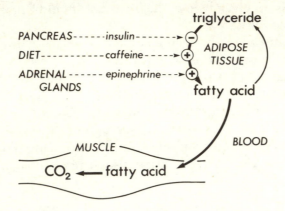

rine in the blood at that time.) The amount ingested should be limited to no more than 5 g of glucose in 100 ml of water (5%) at feeding stations after 15 miles. Even this must be taken with caution, since the blood supply to the intestine is markedly reduced in endurance running, slowing the rate of absorption of glucose. In fact, the higher the concentration of glucose in the drink, the slower its absorption. Too much glucose in the stomach will have an osmotic effect, drawing water from the blood into the stomach and intestine, reducing the blood volume and exacerbating the problem of water loss.

Mobilizing Fat Early The data in Table 4.1 show that the mobilization of fatty acid from fat stores is gradual throughout an endurance run. But there is an artificial way to speed up the mobilization of fatty acids, using caffeine, which mimics the effect of epinephrine on adipose tissue. On the basis of laboratory experiments, Dr. David Costill suggests that a cup of strong black coffee drunk about one to two hours before the race will increase the blood's fatty acid concentration, ensuring that maximal (or near-maximal) rates of fatty acid oxidation occur early in the race. This will conserve glycogen during the early stages of the race making more available for the later stages and so delaying the onset of fatigue.

Setting a Pace The control mechanisms that integrate fatty acid and glucose oxidation will eventually establish a pattern of fuel utilization during the race in which fatty acid, glucose and glycogen oxidation all contribute to ATP formation. Experience enables the marathon runner to optimize these factors subconsciously by setting a pace in tune with the metabolic capacity of the body. Once this pace is established in a race, it is disadvantageous to vary it unless absolutely necessary. Variations in pace will disturb the fuel oxidation pattern, and this will always encourage a greater rate of oxidation of the limited carbohydrate stores.

Glucose After the Race? What the runner does at the end of the race is as important as the careful preparation for the race itself. The race is followed by rest, relaxation and elation at having completed the distance. But the metabolic control systems also relax and this is consequently a dangerous period. The removal of the large energy demand by the now relaxing muscles may decrease the emphasis placed on the control of the blood sugar level by the body, which may therefore become more susceptible to hypoglycemia. In addition, if there has been a serious depletion of blood volume during the race, the readjustment of the cardiovascular system to rest could decrease flow of blood to the brain and so worsen the effects of hypoglycemia. Consequently, the important post-marathon requirements are liquid and carbohydrate. However, just as before the race, simple carbohydrates can be dangerous because they stimulate insulin secretion (since the blood's epinephrine concentration will be reduced after the race has finished). This will lower the blood fatty acid level and force all tissues to use glucose again with possible hypoglycemic consequences. Ideally, the carbohydrate should be complex but in a liquid form to prevent dehydration. Since the body has suddenly stopped generating heat, the ideal post-marathon activity is drinking warm vegetable soup slowly while, if the temperature is low, wrapped in a warm track-suit or blanket.

Somewhat later after the run the body will want to replace potassium lost in sweating. This is very happily done by eating fruit and nuts and drinking fruit juices. It's pleasant to remember that beer also contains considerable amounts of potassium.

5

THE SPRINTER

A sprint is run over a short distance at high speed. In athletic competitions this usually implies distances of from 60 to 100 meters and an average speed of around 23 mph (for the 100 meters). Shorter sprints are demanded from players of sports such as football, baseball, basketball, soccer and rugby but these are also characterized by explosive acceleration, often from a standing start. Sprinters are different from long-distance runners. They are usually larger, have better-developed muscles and are generally younger. They achieve their maximum power output within a few seconds of leaving the blocks. But the sprinter can only maintain this phenomenal power output for very short times. By 200 meters, even an elite sprinter slows. Unlike the marathon runner, the sprinter has no problem with the stores of fuel. Even over a 400 meter sprint, only about 100 grams of carbohydrate will have been consumed, and the sprinter has no use for fat. In fact, it is accumulation of waste products that slows the sprinter.

In this chapter, the extreme specializations of the sprinter's muscle, the means by which ATP is generated and the cause of exhaustion during sprinting are described. By comparing marathon running with sprinting, the metabolic principles that underlie all running modes are explained.

Photo on left   The sprinter

WHAT MAKES SPRINTERS DIFFERENT?

Number and Size of Fibers It is apparent even to the casual observer that the leg muscles of a sprinter are larger than those of a marathon runner. Not only does each muscle possess more fibers, but each fiber has a larger diameter. The first of these factors, the number of fibers in a muscle, is genetically determined: it is established at fertilization by the genes received from the parents. Fiber numbers cannot be altered by environmental factors, so in this sense sprinters are born not made. On the other hand, the number of myofibrils per fiber can be increased by training and so in this sense sprinters are made and not born. The elite sprinters of the world are undoubtedly both born and made—they start life with the potential of a large number of fibers per muscle and increase the size of these fibers by strength-training programs. Why is size so important? Simply because the more muscle that contracts, the greater the power output. Power output is the major factor determining the speed of the sprinter, and power is directly proportional to the cross-sectional area of the muscle.

There is little point in having powerful muscles if they cannot be used effectively. For normal movement, only a proportion of fibers in any one muscle will contract at any one time. The remainder will be pulled passively by the contracting fibers and will not contribute to the power output. For example, when picking up a pen from the desk only a small proportion of the fibers in the arm muscles will contract. Indeed, if all the fibers contracted the power output could be so strong as to damage the muscles. But maximum power must be available when needed, and this requires the simultaneous contraction of all fibers in the muscle so that they all contribute to the power output. Simultaneous contraction is facilitated by motor nerves with large diameters.

Type of Fibers Fiber-typing studies show that the muscles of a sprinter are different in quality as well as quantity. Type IIB fibers, which predominate in the sprinter, have more myofibrils and several times the ATPase activity than do type I fibers. This allows a greater rate of cross-bridge cycling, and so the power output is larger.

TABLE 5.1 FIBER COMPOSITION OF MUSCLE

Animal	Percentage Fiber Composition of Muscle	
	Type I	Type II
Men		
Elite marathon runner	79	21
Middle distance runner	62	38
Sprinters	24	76
Average individual	53	47
Horses		
Quarterhorse	7	93
Thoroughbred	12	88
Heavy hunter	31	69
Dogs		
Greyhound	3	97
Mongrel	31	69

Although it is well-known that the muscles of some sprinters contain nearly 80% of type II fibers, few elite sprinters are prepared to provide biopsy samples of their muscles for scientific study, so that it has not been established whether this is a maximum figure. Certainly the elite sprinters of the animal world can exceed this percentage, as Dr. David Snow of the University of Glasgow has shown by studying the fiber composition of muscles from American Quarterhorses, a breed developed to race over a quarter of a mile, and from greyhounds. In both animals, muscles involved in running were found to contain almost 100% type II fibers.

FUEL FOR THE SPRINT

A major clue to the runner's energy metabolism is provided by analysis of oxygen consumption. In sprinting, a rather surprising fact emerges. During a 100 meter race, less than half a liter of oxygen is consumed, even by a top-class athlete. If metabolism were fully aerobic, as it is for the marathon runner, about ten liters would be used. Why should sprinting be an anaerobic activity? In all probability sprinting evolved as an escape reaction. It requires a violent burst of effort which, hopefully, is maintained for a short time. In earlier times, man would have sprinted to escape from predatory animals. Modern man dashes across the street or runs for the bus. Since we can run 26 or more miles using oxygen to burn fatty acid and glucose, why can't we escape using precisely the same oxidative system?

The answer is another example of the trade-offs that characterize an organism's adaptation to its environment. To provide oxygen at a rate necessary to meet the energy requirements of sprinting would require at least a two-fold increase in the size of arteries and veins and in the number of capillaries. No doubt this could have evolved but it would have decreased the space available for the contractile machinery on which power output depends. In addition, since escape mechanisms must always be available, a large flow of blood would have had to pass through the muscles continuously, so taxing the heart. Aerobic muscles do not suffer from this problem, since their blood supply is much reduced at rest and takes several minutes to increase fully when the muscles are exercised—a delay not acceptable in an escape mechanism! A further trade-off from shifting to anaerobic metabolism is that mitochondria are no longer required and this makes even more space available in the fiber for myofibrils, which means more power and therefore more speed and a greater chance to escape from the predator.

The time has now come to tackle the question of just how ATP is generated without oxygen. Answering this question will reveal what price has to be paid for the benefit of the high power output.

Phosphocreatine: The Small Reserve Tank
If the body could build up a stockpile of ATP in the muscle, this could be used directly as the "fuel" for the escape mechanism. But the body hasn't adopted this elegant plan. Why not? The mechanism for coordinating the rate of ATP production with the rate of utilization depends upon the fiber detecting small changes in the ATP concentration and in adjusting the production rate to maintain a constant or near-constant ATP concentration. In short, this is a feedback control mechanism designed to maintain the concentration of ATP. And even assuming that all the ATP in the muscle could be consumed, it would provide energy for about one second of sprinting.

Evelyn Ashford

—72—

The stockpile approach is such an effective means of providing "immediate" energy that it would be surprising if nature had not adapted it in another guise. Indeed it has. Phosphocreatine, a compound present in muscle at a high concentration, provides an immediate reserve for the resynthesis of ATP. Unlike ATP, phosphocreatine can accumulate at rest and be used during activity. In a single reaction, catalyzed by the enzyme creatine kinase, phosphocreatine phosphorylates ADP to form ATP, and in this way replenishes the ATP used in contraction. After the exercise, phosphocreatine is resynthesized by reversal of the same reaction. Despite its obvious advantage, there is only sufficient phosphocreatine in muscle to provide energy for about 5 seconds of full-speed sprinting (that is, about 50–60 meters). But the great advantage of the phosphocreatine reserve is that it can be used almost instantaneously to regenerate ATP, thus allowing time for the more complex glycolytic control mechanism described below to come into operation.

It is interesting to speculate that in sports that require short sprints lasting no more than a few seconds, as in baseball, football, soccer or rugby, phosphocreatine breakdown may be the major mechanism for replenishing ATP. Rapid acceleration from a standing start and high speed over a short period, so important for some key players in these sports, may be explained by the presence of a large amount of phosphocreatine in their muscles and a high capacity of the enzyme creatine kinase. The phosphocreatine would be repeatedly resynthesized during the quieter periods of the game.

THE SPRINTING LOBSTER

Next time you visit an aquarium, watch the lobsters. They move backwards amazingly fast by a "flick" of their abdomen. For the lobster, this flick represents an escape mechanism, and the fuel used to provide the ATP is phosphoarginine, serving in the lobster the same purpose as phosphocreatine in man. The abdominal muscles of the lobster, so good to eat, have a very low capacity of glycolysis but an enormous activity of the enzyme arginine kinase and about four times more phosphoarginine than there is phosphocreatine in the muscle of man. The lobster is totally dependent upon this fuel for its escape reaction. We speculate that the explosive runners in ball games have a "lobster-like" dependence on phosphocreatine and that all their training is designed to develop this system.

Glycogen: The Large Reserve Tank

If phosphocreatine was the only means of regenerating ATP in sprinting muscle, primitive man, while foraging for food or pursuing other activities, would have been able to stray no more than 50 to 60 meters from safe cover. To overcome this limitation, advantage has been taken of the fact that converting glycogen to lactic acid produces ATP without requiring oxygen. Since a large amount of glycogen is stored in the muscle this extends the distance that can be run at close-to-maximal speed by almost tenfold. By this simple metabolic device the body gains more energy and hence increases endurance in the sprint. But there are two major drawbacks. In the absence of oxygen, each molecule of glucose 1-phosphate produced from

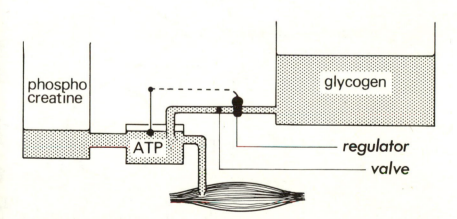

A hydraulic analogy for fuel storage in muscle. The small, but readily available, store of phosphocreatine has been depleted and glycogen is being used.

glycogen is converted, not to pyruvate for entry into the Krebs cycle, but to lactic acid. Unless it can be removed, lactic acid will alter the internal environment of the muscle fiber in such a way as to inhibit further contraction. In short, fatigue and exhaustion set in rapidly. For every glucose unit in glycogen that is converted to lactic acid, very little ATP is produced. Only three molecules of ATP are produced compared with the 39 that would have been produced if it had been fully oxidized to carbon dioxide and water. The solution to this problem is to run glycolysis more rapidly, compensating for the reduced efficiency. Type II fibers can do this. They have a particularly large store of glycogen and high activities of the glycolytic enzymes. Unfortunately, this exacerbates the problem of lactic acid, since to produce sufficient ATP to power contraction, large quantities of lactic acid rapidly accumulate. Nonetheless this must be accepted, since the only metabolic pathway that can produce ATP under anaerobic conditions is the con-

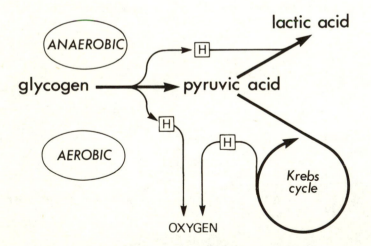

The alternatives. In the absence of oxygen, the reducing equivalents (H) generated by glycolysis are used to convert pyruvic acid to lactic acid. However, when oxygen is available oxidation of the reducing equivalents generates some 13 times more ATP than can be produced from glycogen in the absence of oxygen.

TABLE 5.2   WORLD SPRINT RECORDS

Distance in Meters	Major Fuel	World Record in Seconds	
		Men	Women
100	Phosphocreatine plus glycogen	9.95	10.88
200	Glycogen	19.72	21.72
400	Glycogen plus glucose	43.86	48.60

version of *glycogen* to lactic acid. The blood supply to type IIB fibers is so poor that not enough glucose reaches the muscle to function as a fuel for the sprint.

For 100 meter sprinters, it seems very likely that all the ATP is generated from phosphocreatine degradation plus anaerobic glycolysis. But, for the 200 and especially the 400 meter sprint, the contribution from oxidative processes will increase.

COORDINATING ATP GENERATION WITH ATP UTILIZATION

Every cell in the body, whether a nerve cell in the brain, a type IIB fiber in muscle or a spermatozoon, maintains a constant ATP concentration. ATP is the energy currency of the cell. Unless its concentration is maintained within narrow limits, the cell will suffer a "cash-flow" problem. If services, such as maintaining the correct ion balance and removing water from the cell, cannot be paid for in terms of ATP hydrolysis they will not take place and the energy-bankrupt cell will die. Although the ATP concentration in the cell is small, it can be rapidly regenerated by increasing the rate of fuel oxidation. This means that as soon as the rate of ATP hydrolysis increases, the rate of fuel oxidation must also increase; and that the increase in the latter must match *precisely* the increase in rate of ATP hydrolysis. Let us see what this means for ATP production during sprinting.

At rest, the fiber requires about 0.03 μmole ATP per second per gram of fiber, but in sprinting the demand rises to about 3 μmole per second per gram, a hundredfold increase. Glycolysis now becomes the sole means of ATP generation, and so the rate of glycolysis increases at least a thousandfold from resting. This poses a major problem in control. If the rate of glycolysis was understimulated by only 10% during sprinting, at the end of 10 seconds the ATP concentration in the fibers would have been reduced by half. The fibers would be endangered. Of course, this cannot happen. As the ATP concentration decreases, the cross-bridge cycle is progressively inhibited, causing fatigue, which effectively reduces the rate of ATP utilization.

The Control of Glycolysis

Only two reactions in the whole sequence of enzyme-catalyzed reactions in glycolysis play a role in its control. The first step is the breakdown of glycogen, catalyzed by the enzyme phosphorylase, and the second is one third of the way along the steps in glycolysis at a reaction catalyzed by the enzyme phosphofructokinase. At these sites, two main regulatory agents are at work, although a host of others play minor roles. The reader may remember from Chapter 3 that it is the change in the concentration of calcium ions within the fiber that initiates contraction itself. With typical parsimony, nature uses the same change not only to increase the rate of the cross-bridge cycling but also to increase the activity of phosphorylase, and so increase the rate at which glycogen breaks down.

The concentration of ATP is the second important regulator of glycolysis. When the concentration of ATP falls, even by a very small amount, the enzyme phosphofructokinase works faster and glycolysis increases. Conversely if the concentration of ATP rises, the enzyme slows down. Such a negative feedback mechanism is ideal for maintaining a constant concentration, provided that the mechanism is sensitive to the controlling agent.

In this pathway of glycolysis only about half of the intermediates are named. Each is formed from the previous one by the action of a different enzyme. Control steps are shown with a broken line.

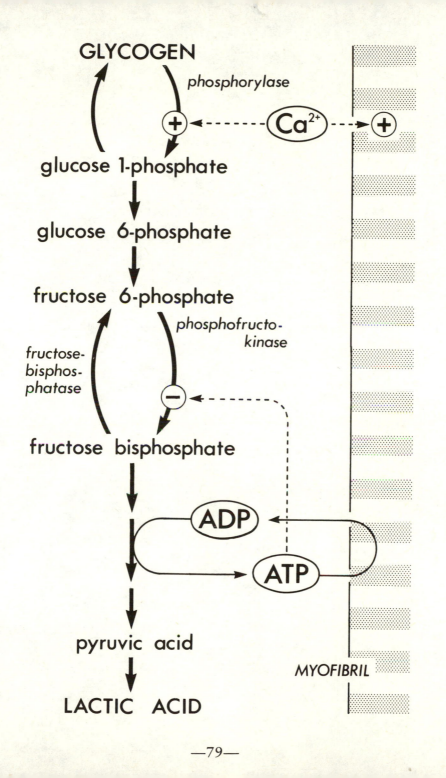

The supreme sensitivity of glycolysis to control by calcium ions and ATP is rather surprisingly achieved by enzymes which catalyze reactions that oppose the specific glycolytic reactions. As a result, both forward and reverse reactions occur simultaneously. For example, phosphofructokinase catalyzes the conversion of fructose 6-phosphate to fructose bisphosphate while the enzyme, fructose bisphosphatase, converts fructose bisphosphate back into fructose 6-phosphate. The simultaneous activity of the two enzymes will result in the cycling of fructose 6-phosphate to fructose bisphosphate and back. No net glycolytic reaction takes place, yet ATP is hydrolyzed to ADP and phosphate. This means that the chemical energy in ATP is converted into heat which is eventually lost from the body. For this reason the mechanism is sometimes termed a futile cycle. But it is far from purposeless.

Just how a substrate cycle operates to increase the sensitivity of control is complicated. But what is important here is to appreciate that sensitivity increases as the activities of *both* of the enzymes involved increase. The role of the cycle is best explained by reference to the sprinter's behavior immediately before an important 100 meter race. Resting in the dressing room before the race, the rate of glycolysis in the muscles will be low, as will be the activities of both phosphofructokinase and fructose bisphosphatase. Consequently, the cycling rate and therefore the sensitivity of the system to changes in concentration of ATP will also be low. Now the race approaches. The anxiety level rises. And then when the sprinter is on the blocks waiting for the gun, nervous tension and anticipation result in the secretion of high levels of the stress hormones, epinephrine and norepinephrine. In the muscle, these hormones lead to rapid activation of *both* phosphofructokinase and fructose bisphosphatase. Although the flux through glycolysis remains low, since the race has not yet started, the rate of cycling is now high so that when the gun fires and the sprint starts, the control system is very sensitive to small changes in concentration of ATP and the other regulators. A similar cycle also exists at the phosphorylase reaction which increases its sensitivity to calcium ions.

A high school hurdler. Is epinephrine working for him?

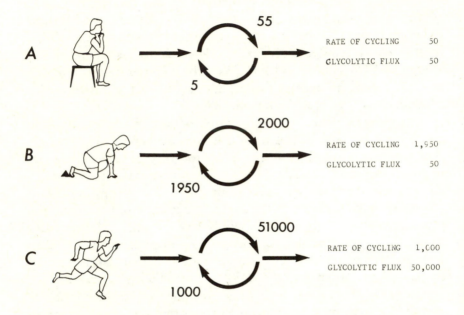

A	RATE OF CYCLING 50
	GLYCOLYTIC FLUX 50
B	RATE OF CYCLING 1,950
	GLYCOLYTIC FLUX 50
C	RATE OF CYCLING 1,000
	GLYCOLYTIC FLUX 50,000

Changes in the rate of cycling and flux through glycolysis which might occur A) before a 100m sprint, B) at the start of the 100m sprint, and C) during a 100m sprint. The upper arrow represents the enzyme phosphofructokinase and the lower arrow the enzyme fructose bisphosphatase. The flux is the difference between the rates of the forward and reverse reactions.

These sensitive control mechanisms ensure a smooth transition from the use of phosphocreatine to the use of glycogen to power the sprint. The importance of nervous tension in 100 meter sprinters is well known and was aptly emphasized by the trainer Sam Mussabini in the film *"Chariots of Fire"*. Mussabini, explaining to Harold Abrahams that he can beat Eric Liddell over the short sprint, says: "a short sprint is run on nerves; it's tailor-made for neurotics". In the 1924 Olympic Games, Abrahams won the 100 yard sprint and Liddell won the 440 yard race.

CAUSES OF FATIGUE

Fatigue can clearly be seen in the finishing stages of a 400 meter race. The power output fails, and despite every effort and exhortation, the runner slows. As in distance running, fatigue is a warning that the muscles are no longer able to perform the task demanded of them. Otherwise, they will be damaged. But is fatigue in sprinting caused by the very same mechanism as in endurance running—depletion of muscle glycogen reserves with consequent decrease in the rate of ATP generation? The answer is *no*. During all-out sprinting, fatigue is detectable after about 20 seconds, although muscle glycogen stores could provide ATP for at least 80 seconds of sprinting. Direct measurements on the muscles of volunteers exhausted by sprinting show that considerable glycogen is still present in the muscles.

TABLE 5.3 A MEASURE OF FATIGUE

SUBSTANCE	CONCENTRATION OF FUELS (μmol PER g FRESH MUSCLE)	
	Muscle at Rest	Muscle Immediately after Exhaustive Sprinting
Glycogen	88	58
Phosphocreatine	17.0	3.7
ATP	4.6	3.4
Lactate	1.1	30.5
pH	7.1	6.3

Lactic Acid Lactic acid is so named because it is produced from milk by the action of bacteria on milk sugar, lactose. Lactic acid is responsible for the sour taste in soured milk. The bacteria produce lactic acid from the sugar by exactly the same process as in muscle—anaerobic glycolysis. Like all acids, it can dissociate to produce a positively charged hydrogen ion, H^+ (known as a proton), and a negatively charged ion, in this case a lactate ion. Under conditions in the cell, this dissociation (or ionization) is virtually complete, according to the equation:

$$\text{lactic acid} \rightarrow H^+ + \text{lactate}^-$$

When the athletic commentator graphically describes the sprint to the finish line by saying that the athlete finishes "in a sea of lactic acid" it is not the lactic acid nor the lactate that causes problems but the protons that result from the dissociation.

Protons readily combine with negatively charged ions, including those present in proteins, as follows:

$$\text{protein}^- + H^+ \rightarrow \text{protein-H}$$

Many proteins have special functions in the cell (such as catalysis) which depend on them being in a particular state of ionization. In the presence of protons this state is altered so that their function is impaired, in some cases irreversibly. The importance of protons is emphasized by the simple fact that we have enough muscle glycogen and a sufficient capacity of anaerobic glycolysis to produce a massive quantity of protons—sufficient to kill ourselves in less than one minute. Fortunately fatigue prevents us from committing suicide.

Protons and Buffers Those readers who remember high school chemistry will be aware of the pH scale which provides a simple and quantitative measure of the proton concentration. Somewhat illogically, as the proton concentration increases the pH decreases. A calculation shows that during an exhaustive 400 meter race, enough protons would be produced from the conversion of glycogen to lactic acid to lower the pH of the blood and

SPRINTING AND THE HUNTER

The limited duration of the escape mechanisms also applies to animals in the wild and for centuries the hunter has taken advantage of this knowledge. When exhaustion occurs prey can be easily taken. Perhaps one of the earliest references to the behavior of "sprinting" animals was given by Xenophon in Anabasis, written in about 400 B.C. Xenophon tells the story of the expedition which Cyrus the younger led against his brother Artaxerxes II, king of Persia, in the hope of gaining for himself the Persian throne. In order to obtain food for the army, the Greeks had to be aware of the behavior of their quarry. Xenophon recounts how "the bustards on the other hand can be caught if one is quick in starting them up, for they fly only short distances, like partridges, and soon tire; and their flesh was delicious". The behavior of the bustard, a heavy bird related to the crane, so well described by Xenophon, can now be explained in biochemical terms. The accumulation of protons in the pectoral muscles of the bustards enabled the Greek army to eat and hence survive.

Another example of the ease with which white muscle can be exhausted is known to every fisherman. Once having a fish on the hook, an angler knows it is impossible to land it immediately. The power of the fish might break the line or even the rod. Instead the angler "plays" his fish after hooking it. During this time the violent swimming of the fish exhausts the substantial amount of white muscle in its body. Eventually, this muscle can no longer contract (due to the accumulation of protons in the muscle and the consequent decrease in pH) and only the thin lines of red muscle oppose the angler and at last the fish can be landed. One could speculate that if all the muscle fibers in the fish were red (type I), the angler would have to wait all day and possibly all night to land his catch! Hunters in the animal world also exploit the limited duration of the escape reaction. Hunting dogs, for example, work in a pack so they can take turns to chase the prey to exhaustion.

muscle to below pH 2.0. But measurements show that the muscle pH actually falls from pH 7.0 to about pH 6.0, and that of the blood from pH 7.4 to about pH 6.9. Is our chemistry wrong? No, because there exist in the body compounds known as buffers, which "mop up" protons and so reduce the extent of a pH change. They do this because they can combine readily with protons when the proton concentration is high, and release them when it is low. They act rather like a sponge which can "mop up" water spilt on to the table and release it when squeezed into the sink. More chemically, buffer action can be represented by an equilibrium in which A represents the buffer:

$$A^- + H^+ \rightleftharpoons AH$$

The direction of this reaction depends on the concentration of protons.

Without buffers in muscle and blood, we could not sprint for more than five or six seconds. But there aren't many chemicals in the muscle that can act as buffers. Consequently, protons produced in the muscle diffuse into the blood, where the buffering capacity is greater. As a result, a much larger amount of lactic acid can be produced, a faster pace achieved and endurance increased.

A simple demonstration of the relationship between bloodflow and fatigue can be carried out as you sit reading this book. Raise your right arm above your head and allow your left arm to hang down. The blood flow to your right hand will be worse than to your left because of the extra work needed to pump blood against the pull of gravity. In all other respects your hands are likely to be similar (to check that this is so the demonstration can be repeated a little later with the hands reversed). Now open and close both hands at the same rate repeatedly and rapidly. After less than a minute the muscles in your right forearm and hand will feel distinctly weary while those on your left side will be much less tired.

The protons, once they enter the bloodstream, meet one of the most important buffers in the body, the hydrogencarbonate ion (also known as bicarbonate). It combines with a proton to form a molecule of carbonic acid:

$$HCO_3^- + H^+ \rightarrow H_2CO_3$$

This buffer system, fortunately, is much more efficient than would appear from this reaction. The product of the reaction between hydrogencarbonate and protons, carbonic acid, is broken down in the bloodstream and in the lungs to produce carbon dioxide and water:

$$H_2CO_3 \rightarrow H_2O + CO_2$$

The complete buffer reaction can therefore be described as follows:

$$HCO_3^- + H^+ \rightarrow H_2CO_3 \rightarrow CO_2 + H_2O$$

These are the same reactions that decrease the proton concentration (the acidity) of the stomach when a solution of bicarbonate of soda or "Alka-Seltzer" is taken after 'over-indulgence'; the gas produced is of course carbon dioxide. The system is *more* efficient in the bloodstream because of the presence of an enzyme, carbonic anhydrase, which speeds up the formation of carbon dioxide.

The reason that we can run more than about 100 meters depends to a large extent on the efficiency of this system and especially the response of two other organs in the body—the kidney and lungs. First, when the proton concentration in the blood increases, the kidney secretes some protons into the urine and at the same time hydrogencarbonate ions into the blood—this is equivalent to taking bicarbonate of soda. In addition, the rate of breathing increases, which removes carbon dioxide from the lungs, and this speeds up its diffusion from the blood to the air across the alveolar membrane. Increasing the rate at which hydrogencarbonate ions are added to the blood and the rate at which carbon dioxide is removed will allow the buffer system to "mop up" more protons and "lose" them as carbon dioxide and water. In this way the body quickly and efficiently brings under control an otherwise lethal rate of proton production.

Protons and Fatigue

How does an increase in proton concentration in muscle result in fatigue? At the molecular level, the cause of fatigue is probably identical to that in marathon running—a decrease in the rate of cross-bridge cycling. There are at least two theories to explain how this is brought about by protons.

TABLE 5.4   LIMITATIONS FOR THE SPRINTER

Time of Sprint (Seconds)	Fuel Used	Limitation for Performance
0–4	Phosphocreatine	Catalytic activity of the enzyme creatine kinase (see Fig. 5.3)
3–6	Phosphocreatine plus glycogen	Control of key enzymes in glycolysis to provide a thousandfold increase in rate of process
6–10	Muscle glycogen	Glycolytic capacity of muscle
10–20	Muscle glycogen	Glycolytic capacity of muscle plus buffering capacity to decrease the accumulation of protons
20–40	Muscle glycogen	Buffering capacity and bloodflow to decrease the accumulation of protons Exhaustion at pH 6.0–0.000001 g per liter of protons

Protons, like calcium ions, are positively charged. Calcium ions control the rate of cross-bridge cycling by making binding sites available on the thin filaments for the cross-bridges to attach. Protons can interfere with this process. They prevent calcium ions from binding to the regulatory protein on the thin filament. This interference will reduce the power output by the muscle. But how can we explain the discomfort and pain that accompany fatigue? We know that protons escape from the muscle and pass into the space between the muscle, before entering the bloodstream to be buffered by the hydrogencarbonate system. If sensory receptors, embedded between the muscle fibers, can detect an increase in proton concentration, they might then increase the frequency of nerve signals to the brain. These signals would be interpreted by the brain as pain.

In Chapter 4 we saw that fatty acid oxidation can lead to a decrease in the rate of glycolysis by increasing the effectiveness of ATP as a regulator of key enzymes in glycolysis. Protons can do exactly the same thing. As the proton concentration increases, the rate of glycolysis decreases. This is a feedback inhibition mechanism which prevents a dangerous and even lethal accumulation of protons.

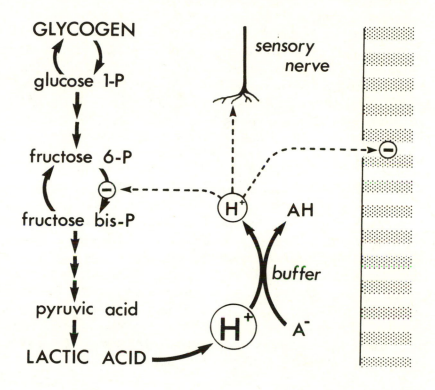

Although the concentration of protons produced by glycolysis is reduced by buffering, enough protons remain to cause fatigue (broken lines).

THE PSYCHIATRIST'S COUCH

Tiredness and a lack of energy is a common complaint of many patients in the physician's consulting room. If the patient complains frequently but shows no signs of muscular or cardiovascular disease, a visit to the psychiatrist may be recommended. But is the patient really suffering from a psychiatric disturbance or is it a case of fatigue due to proton accumulation in the muscles? It is difficult for the average physician to test for proton accumulation without resorting to detailed and expensive physiological and biochemical testing. A deficiency, even a partial deficiency, of one of the many proteins involved in the Krebs cycle would force the muscles of the patient to rely more on conversion of glycogen to lactic acid, with the consequent accumulation of protons and hence the danger of fatigue upon physical exertion. The pain would be real and not imagined! A partial deficiency, which might not have a serious effect during youth, could cause problems as middle age approaches since the aerobic capacity of muscle decreases with age. A history of fatigue, tiredness and pain only arising in the middle years of life—the same time as problems of a more general nature arise—is a recipe for the psychiatrist's chair.

The application of a new technique, nuclear magnetic resonance spectroscopy, may make the diagnosis of such cases much easier, for the patient would only have to insert a limb into a machine and carry out some exercises. And the cure would be easy too: a slow but gradual training schedule to maintain the aerobic capacity of the muscle in its youthful state.

RUNNING OTHER DISTANCES

Our discussion of running has focused on the two extremes—marathon running and sprinting. Sadly, much less biochemical information is available for middle distance running, but four points arise from our discussions.

- When running from a "cold" start it takes several minutes for the blood flowing to the leg muscles to flow faster. Indeed, the increase in blood flow to a large group of muscles must occur gradually. Sudden vasodilation may result in a catastrophic fall in blood pressure with the risk of fainting or worse. During this time, anaerobic conversion of glycogen to lactic acid must provide a significant proportion of the ATP required. This is a disadvantage, since lactic acid production will use up some of the limited glycogen stores; and it will also make use of the buffering capacity to remove protons. Runners, wanting to facilitate the flow of blood to the large muscles, "warm up" before a race, exercising to encourage premature vasodilation in the muscles that will be used during the race. Some runners use relaxation exercises to maintain this vasodilation since stress and anxiety immediately before the start of the race can cause vasoconstriction in the muscles.

- Runners of middle distances, below about 3,000 meters, probably make use of both aerobic and anaerobic processes. Glucose will be completely oxidized via Krebs cycle but in addition some glycogen will be degraded to lactic acid. Some lactic acid production can occur without the risk of fatigue, since the better blood supply in middle distance runners will allow continuous removal of lactic acid into the blood where it can be effectively buffered. This will allow type IIB fibers to contribute to the power output of the middle distance runner. Since type IIB fibers have a greater power output than type I fibers it may be advantageous for middle distance runners to possess muscles with both type I and type II fibers. The very few fiber typing studies on such runners confirm this view (Table 5.1).

- It is a characteristic of some elite middle and long-distance runners that they can run very close to their maximal oxidative capacity, perhaps, at 90% of their $V_{O_2 max}$, without producing lactic acid. By reference to page 76 the reader should be able to appreciate that when pyruvate is produced from glucose it can either be converted to lactic acid—the inefficient pathway—or enter Krebs cycle for complete oxidation—the efficient pathway. If oxygen is available the latter is obviously preferable. This can only be achieved if rates of glycolysis and Krebs cycle are almost perfectly coordinated. Such coordination is probably improved by training.

It should now be clear to the reader that as the speed of a runner increases towards the maximum aerobic capacity, a point will be reached when lactic acid production increases markedly. Some scientists believe that there is a specific speed, or a specific percentage of the $\dot{V}O_{2\,max}$, at which this rate of lactic acid production markedly increases; it is known as the anaerobic threshold or onset of blood lactate accumulation (OBLA). OBLA is useful in predicting an elite runner—one who can run at a very high percentage of $\dot{V}O_{2\,max}$ before lactic acid begins to increase. Unfortunately, this is controversial. Other scientists consider that there is no threshold for lactic acid accumulation, arguing that a gradual increase in lactic acid production occurs as the $\dot{V}O_{2\,max}$ is approached. Only further research will give us an answer to this important question.

• The final 200 to 400 meters of a middle or long distance race usually becomes a sprint, so that the demand for ATP exceeds the aerobic capacity of the muscles and the ATP is then produced from both the Krebs cycle and glycogen degradation to lactic acid. A high rate of glycolysis will result in the accumulation of protons in the muscle and cause fatigue, as in the sprinter. The important point for the runner, once again, is the relative inefficiency of anaerobic glycolysis for ATP production and hence the need to restrict the final sprint till as late as possible.

THE SEDENTARY NON-RUNNER

The average unfit person can still run to catch a bus or train but cannot run even one mile at a steady pace. Why is this? A sedentary lifestyle results in a marked decrease in the capacity of the Krebs cycle and in the number of mitochondria, especially in the early stages of middle age (mid-thirties). Although the capacity of the Krebs cycle diminishes, the glycolytic capacity remains at a normal level. The unfit person comes to rely almost entirely on anaerobic glycolysis to provide ATP for running, and probably accumulates as much lactic acid at 5 miles per hour as the trained sprinter does at 25 miles per hour, so that exhaustion occurs quickly. Can anything be done about it? Yes, and endurance training is the answer. Slowly at first, but frequently, so that the stimulus for the activities of the enzymes of Krebs cycle to increase is presented to the muscle every day. Gradually and progressively the aerobic capacity will return and its efficiency, in terms of converting glucose and fatty acid into ATP, will be felt by the runner. At first, one mile, then two, three, four, five . . . all without fatigue, until eventually, the New York marathon beckons and the runner can return with renewed interest to Chapter 4.

6

THE RUNNER'S HEART AND LUNGS

Just as an army is dependent upon the strength of its supply lines so the muscles of the body are dependent on their supply of fuels and oxygen. Attention must be given to maintaining the capacity of these supply lines and for that it helps to have an understanding of the machinery itself. In all vertebrates, the supply problem has been solved by a transport system in which fuels and oxygen are carried in the blood through a network of closed tubes, reaching all tissues of the body.

TRANSPORTING GASES

Oxygen dissolves in water, but only to a very limited extent; about 2.0 ml per liter at body temperature. Thanks to hemoglobin, this value is increased in blood by a factor of one hundred. All the hemoglobin is contained in the red cells. There are more than a hundred million red cells in a drop of human blood.

It is vital for the runner that as many hemoglobin molecules as possible are loaded with oxygen as the blood passes through the lungs and are unloaded as it passes through the muscles. This happens automatically; loading occurs when the concentration of free oxygen is high and unloading when it is low.

More oxygen could be carried in the blood if it contained more red cells. Knowing how important oxygen transport is to the work

Photo on left   Greg Meyer, who won the Boston marathon in 1983, shown here in the Cascade Runoff, 1981.

of muscle during sustained running, we would expect the runner's red blood cell count to rise. But it doesn't. If the proportion of the blood taken up by red blood cells (the hematocrit) rises above the normal value (around 45%), the viscosity of the blood would increase too, making the heart work harder both at rest and during running. In fact, the total blood volume rises, which of course increases the number of red cells without increasing the hematocrit.

Not only does the blood transport oxygen; it also removes carbon dioxide from the tissues. Carbon dioxide is much more soluble in water than is oxygen, but not soluble enough for its rapid removal from tissues. This time the answer to the problem is different. The carbon dioxide is converted to a form that is soluble. Carbon dioxide reacts with water to form, first, carbonic acid and then hydrogencarbonate ions, which are very soluble:

$$H_2O + CO_2 \rightarrow H_2CO_3 \rightarrow H^+ + HCO_3^-$$

In the lungs, the reverse reactions occur. Hydrogencarbonate ions are converted to carbon dioxide which diffuses into the air in the lungs and is breathed out of the body. The formation of hydrogencarbonate ions has one further advantage. It is accompanied by a production of protons (H^+) which bind to hemoglobin and weaken the binding between it and oxygen. As the muscle works harder and produces more carbon dioxide, and so more protons, more oxygen is automatically released from the hemoglobin for use by the muscle.

INTERFACE WITH THE ENVIRONMENT

Some 20% of the air surrounding us is oxygen but to reach the blood it must pass through our outer surface. Some animals, like worms, possess a skin which is permeable to oxygen. This however would not be satisfactory for large, active, warm-blooded animals like man. The rate of diffusion of gas through a membrane is slow unless the membrane is thin; unfortunately a thin membrane offers little protection from the external environment. Diffusion is also speeded up by increasing the area over which it can take place, but the external surface area of an animal is limited. These problems

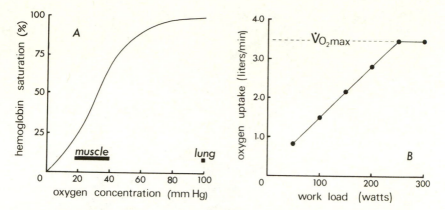

A) This graph shows that when the blood leaves the lungs, virtually all the hemoglobin is in the form of oxyhemoglobin. The S-shaped nature of the curve ensures that oxygen is effectively unloaded at the concentration of oxygen present in working muscles. B) As the work load increases so does the oxygen uptake until the maximum aerobic capacity ($\dot{V}_{O_2\,max}$) is reached. Additional work is only possible because of anaerobic metabolism.

have been solved by the evolution of lungs, which are essentially very extensive invaginations into the body of a thin surface membrane. In humans, this would occupy approximately 50 square meters, that is, thirty times the area of the skin, or the floor space of a large dining-room. Furthermore, an internal surface can more easily be kept moist, thus aiding gas diffusion, without too great a danger of water loss by evaporation. The respiratory surface consists of millions of tiny sacs each of which receives a branch from the main airway and is in intimate contact with capillary vessels. The whole system is condensed into two structures, known as the lungs, which reside in the chest. Changes in chest volume, caused by contraction and relaxation of the diaphragm and intercostal muscles, flush air in and out of the airways. During its brief stay in the lungs the oxygen content of the air falls from 21% to about 14.5% while that of carbon dioxide rises from almost zero to 5.5%.

Vital Capacity The maximum usable volume of the lungs, defined as the vital capacity, is measured by taking the deepest possible breath and expelling the air as completely as possible into a device for measuring its volume. Vital capacity depends on age,

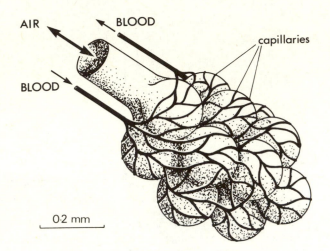

AIR

BLOOD

BLOOD

capillaries

0·2 mm

An air-sac showing the intimate contact with capillaries carrying blood.

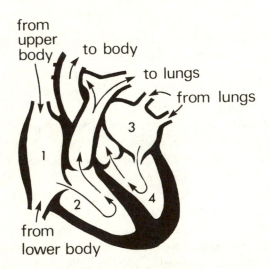

from
upper
body

to body

to lungs

from lungs

3

1

2

4

from
lower body

The working of the heart is best understood by following the route taken by blood during a single heartbeat. Blood returning from the body enters the right atrium (1). As this collecting chamber contracts, blood is squeezed into the right ventricle (2). Fractionally later, this too contracts, sending blood out of the heart towards the lungs. Oxygenated blood returns from the lungs to the left atrium (3) and then into the left ventricle (4) from which it is pumped around the body. Both the left and the right sides of the heart contact simultaneously. The flow of blood in the wrong direction is prevented by valves.

size, sex and general pulmonary health and is usually within the range 3.5 to 6 liters. Endurance runners are usually found in the upper limit of this range which is probably an effect of training. In normal breathing only about 0.5 liters is drawn in and out; this amount (one breath) is known as the tidal volume and is repeated about 15 times per minute.

Runners may want to increase the amount of air drawn into the lungs, in order to increase the volume of oxygen available to the blood as it flows through the lungs, ensuring that as much hemoglobin as possible is fully loaded. The volume of air drawn into the lungs can be increased either by increasing the volume per breath or the number of breaths per minute. If you multiply the tidal volume by the number of breaths taken per minute, the minute volume is obtained. Minute volumes greater than 120 liters can occur for prolonged periods in endurance runners but such volumes would occur in untrained men only for very short periods. Training not only increases the maximal minute volume that can be achieved, it also increases the efficiency of gas exchange (of both oxygen and carbon dioxide) across the membranes of the lungs and blood capillaries, so that a given speed of running can be maintained with a smaller minute volume. In long-distance races, the minute volume is not the factor limiting oxygen supply to the muscles but in middle-distance races it may be.

At rest we hardly notice our breathing and this is not surprising since we use less than 1% of our energy in this activity, but in a long, hard race this can rise to 10%—and breathing becomes very noticeable.

Aerobic Capacity

A physiological parameter often encountered in running literature, and much studied by exercise physiologists, is the aerobic capacity, known by the abbreviation $VO_{2\,max}$. This is the maximum volume of oxygen (not air) that can be used (not merely taken into the lungs) per minute by an individual. Since large people will have higher aerobic capacities than small people, aerobic capacity is usually reported per kilogram body weight. Endurance athletes usually have high aerobic capacities; an average value for a normal 20 year old man is 45 ml per kg per minute, whereas many endurance runners have values above 70 and some elite runners over 80 or even 90 ml per kg per minute.

Aerobic Capacity and Mount Everest The ability to maintain a high power output for a long period of time, which demands aerobic metabolism, is required of mountaineers as well as runners. Until 1978, Everest had only been climbed with the help of supplementary oxygen. On May 8th, 1978 Peter Habeler and Reinhold Messner reached the summit of Everest without supplementary oxygen for the first time. It has been estimated that the values of $\dot{V}_{O_2 max}$ for these mountaineers were above 70 ml per kg per minute whereas Himalayan mountaineers of the 1950s and 1960s had values of $\dot{V}_{O_2 max}$ of only about 50 ml per kg per minute. Perhaps Habeler and Messner could have been Olympic champion distance runners had they not been mountaineers!

$\dot{V}_{O_2 max}$ and Training Aerobic capacity increases on training (from 15–60%) but decreases with increasing age. It might be expected that the athlete with the highest $\dot{V}_{O_2 max}$ will be the best endurance runner. If that were true, a simple physiological measurement could select potential Olympic champions. Values of $\dot{V}_{O_2 max}$ are important but a further factor complicates the picture. This factor is the percentage of the $\dot{V}_{O_2 max}$ that can be attained in prolonged running without stimulating anaerobic glycolysis, which would rapidly cause fatigue.

Some elite distance runners are able to utilize as much as 90% of their $\dot{V}_{O_2 max}$ for most or all of a marathon race but most distance runners use only about 75–80% of their's. Above this value, fatigue occurs rapidly, due probably to the accumulation of lactic acid.

MOVING THE BLOOD

Although it is only one component of the circulatory system, the heart understandably receives the most attention; if it stops we stop—permanently. Basically the heart is a muscular bag fitted with valves so that blood enters one end and is periodically squeezed out of the other. Indeed, the heart of an insect is little more than this and serves to swirl the "blood" around the organs. Vertebrates, in contrast, have a closed circulation system in which the blood flows out of the heart through arteries to the tissues,

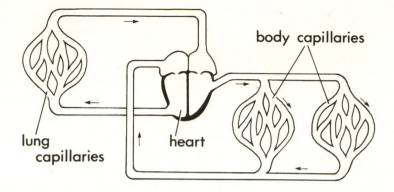

Capillary beds in each organ of the body are arranged in parallel so that blood only flows through one in the course of a single circulation.

where it is distributed through capillaries, and then back to the heart through veins.

To someone who has not studied biology, the heart seems to be a complex organ, but it is really only a pair of pumps neatly packaged together. Blood returning from the body through the veins fills the right atrium and is squeezed through to the right ventricle before being pumped out along the pulmonary arteries to the lungs, where oxygenation occurs. The blood, at a lower pressure, now returns to the second pump, on the left side of the heart, where a similar process occurs. As the left ventricle empties, a process known as systole, the pressure in the aorta rises, distending its elastic walls. As this pressure rises it forces blood towards the capillaries and the pressure falls. The minimum pressure occurs as the heart refills and is known as the diastolic pressure. Because of the elastic walls of the aorta and other arteries, the jerky flow of blood produced by a pumping heart is to some extent evened out, but nonetheless a pressure wave is transmitted along the main arteries at each stroke of the left ventricle. This is the pulse, it can be detected at the wrist and other places where a major artery passes near the surface of the body. The pulse rate is of course equal to the heart rate, but in practice is easier to measure.

Vasoconstriction and Vasodilation
The finer branches of the arteries are called arterioles. Their walls have less elastic tissue but more smooth muscle, arranged in a circular fashion, so

that contraction of this muscle reduces the diameter of the vessel and hence the bloodflow. Contraction of the arterioles is known as vasoconstriction. The diameter of the arterioles can also be widened, allowing blood to flow more quickly and in greater volume. This is called vasodilation. Vasoconstriction or vasodilation can occur independently in each tissue of the body, so that the blood supply to any part of the body can be regulated independently.

Running causes vasodilation in the active muscles, thus increasing their supply of fuel and oxygen. Sudden vasodilation at the onset of running can reduce the blood pressure; there is then a danger that the runner will collapse. Fortunately, compensatory vasoconstriction of the blood flow to the intestine, liver and kidney allows the blood pressure to be maintained.

Urban life in the post-industrial age is not entirely stress-free, and we know that today a large proportion of the population suffers from high blood pressure (hypertension). Epinephrine, the stress hormone, causes vasoconstriction in some tissues. The blood pressure must then increase to force blood through these tissues. Relaxation exercises, meditation or yoga all reduce stress and with it blood pressure, probably by preventing vasoconstriction in peripheral arterioles. The anxiety and stress before an important race causes vasoconstriction in some muscles. After a few minutes running, the release of vasodilatory compounds from the fibers overcomes this vasoconstriction, allowing the full flow of blood to the muscle. Prevention of the vasoconstriction by relaxation exercises *before* a race permits muscles to oxidize glucose from the very start of the race and this conserves muscle glycogen some of which otherwise would have been degraded to lactic acid to provide energy before vasodilation occurs.

Runner's Diarrhea

The unpleasant phenomenon of runner's diarrhea can be explained by vasoconstriction in the intestine. If the vasoconstriction is severe, due to a massive vasodilation in the muscles and the skin (for cooling), and due also to dehydration, the blood supply to the intestine will be very limited. This can deprive the tissue of oxygen and hence cause a deficiency of energy in the cells that line the lumen of the large intestine. Approximately 300 ml of fluid enters the intestinal lumen every hour and normally 98% of the fluid that enters the lumen is reabsorbed, so that about

200 ml is normally lost in 24 hours in the feces. However, absorption of water is an energy-requiring process and failure to absorb this water due to lack of energy in the cells, will result in a massive increase in fluid in the intestine and hence diarrhea, which will exacerbate the dehydration of the runner.

Capillaries

Capillaries are quite different from arterioles. Not only are they very narrow, they are also very short (around 0.5 millimeters), and it has been calculated that a single red blood cell spends little more than one second passing through a capillary. In each tissue, many capillaries are arranged in parallel so that oxygen diffuses only a short distance to reach any cell.

Blood from the capillaries flows through venules into veins where the pressure is much lower. In fact, the pressure in the veins is so low that the return of blood from the lower limbs to the heart, against the pull of gravity, can be sluggish. This could (and occasionally does) lead to problems as blood accumulates in distended veins in the lower limbs and is not available for recirculation to vital organs, such as the brain. For instance, when an upright stance in a person is maintained for long periods without any muscle movement that person may faint. Fainting is an inelegant but effective way of reducing the hydrostatic pressure in lower limb veins. The problem is normally prevented by simple pocket valves in the major veins which permit flow of blood toward the heart only. During exercise these veins are "massaged" by surrounding muscles so that blood flow is assisted.

Cardiac Output

The volume of the blood that leaves the heart in a given time (the cardiac output) is increased by running. An increased cardiac output can be achieved in two ways: by increasing heart rate or by increasing the volume of blood expelled per beat, that is, the stroke volume.

The largest change in an untrained subject is the increase in heart rate; in trained athletes the largest change is in stroke volume. By endurance training, stroke volume is increased almost twofold. This is achieved not only by enlargement of the heart, due to increased size of the muscle fibers, but also by a more complete emptying on each contraction. As a result, the athlete's heart is more efficient, as more blood is pumped during each contraction.

This is true both during running or at rest. The basal heart rate (taken first thing in the morning before any exercise) of an elite endurance runner can be lower than 35 beats per minute compared with twice that number in an untrained person.

Blood Doping The ability to improve performance by increasing the hemoglobin content of the blood is known as blood doping or blood boosting, a phenomenon that won public attention during recent Olympic Games.

An important question for the middle distance runner (and the exercise physiologist) is what limits the rate of ATP generation in the muscle: cardiac output, availability of fuels, mitochondrial capacity for oxidative metabolism, or oxygen uptake? Only if oxygen uptake was the limiting factor would blood doping be beneficial, since it would increase the concentration of oxygen in the capillaries and so increase the rate of diffusion into the muscle. Under normal circumstances it is unlikely that cardiac output is limiting; fuel supply is limiting probably only in marathon running or ultradistance running, but it has been unclear whether mitochondrial capacity or oxygen uptake is limiting for other distances. Laboratory experiments on blood doping suggest it is oxygen uptake.

Blood doping involves the removal of about 1 liter of blood from an athlete, and its storage in a frozen state (in the presence of

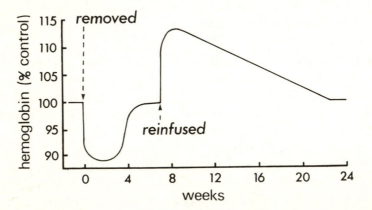

This graph shows changes in the hemoglobin content of male subjects after 900 milliliters (about 1½ pints) of blood had been removed, stored for seven weeks and reinfused.

glycerol to protect the red cells). After removal of the blood, the total number of red cells and therefore the amount of hemoglobin is reduced. The body adapts by increasing the rate of production of red blood cells so that after about five weeks the number of cells and the amount of hemoglobin has returned to normal. At this time, the frozen blood is thawed and reinfused into the athlete. This increases the total number of red cells and the amount of hemoglobin by about 10%. Experimental studies have shown that soon after reinfusion the $Vo_{2\,max}$ is increased by about 5%, as is endurance capacity. For competitive athletes a difference of 5% easily covers the margin between winning and losing.

CONTROLLING THE CHANGES

The beneficial effects of training on the cardiovascular and indeed the muscular systems are not achieved overnight, as any jogger who has decided to train for a marathon will confirm. These effects are described in Chapter 7, but we are concerned here with the normal control mechanisms that adjust the response of the cardiovascular system very quickly and very effectively when exercise begins. How is this achieved? Much of the control system depends upon nerves but this is supplemented, usually at a local level, by chemicals. In general, sensory receptors are present at certain sites in the body and these relay information to the brain, via sensory nerves, concerning conditions at that particular site. A number of centers in the brain coordinate incoming signals and then send out appropriate signals to the heart, blood vessels and respiratory muscles. Both the nervous and chemical control mechanisms involve the principle of negative feedback, that is, a change from a set level causes a response that tends to return the system to the original level.

Rhythmic contraction is a unique property of cardiac muscle. Even if the heart is removed from all nervous and chemical contact with the body, it will continue to contract rhythmically, provided it has a source of fuel and oxygen. This rhythmicity is generated from one specific region of the heart, known as the pacemaker. The pacemaker determines the basic heart rhythm. It alone produces a high rate of contractions, but the rate is modified by nervous signals from a specific center in the brain, the cardiovascular center. Two nervous pathways connect this center with the heart; impulses passing along the vagus nerve cause the pacemaker to slow the heart rate while those reaching the heart via the sympathetic nerve cause an increase in rate.

The cardiovascular center receives information concerning the blood pressure from receptors in two major arteries, the aorta, and that which provides the main blood supply to the brain, the carotid. When the blood pressure in either of these areas decreases, the heart rate is increased. Heart rate is also controlled, via the cardiovascular center, by higher centers of the brain. For example, fear, anxiety or, of importance to the runner, anticipation of exercise will raise the heart rate. Finally, evidence has recently been obtained that the cardiovascular center receives signals, probably nervous, from the exercising muscles themselves, but the nervous pathway, and the change in the muscle that initiates such signals, is not known.

From this discussion it should be clear that to control vital functions, the body has evolved a series of control mechanisms which operate in concert so that they normally complement one another. If one mechanism fails to operate the other becomes more important; for example, if both sets of nerves from the cardiovascular center to the heart are cut or blocked, the heart still responds appropriately to severe exercise. It does this not by increasing heart rate but by increasing stroke volume.

The flow of blood through resting muscles is very low but, at the onset of running, vasodilation occurs which results in an increase in flow of blood to the exercising muscles. If only this change occurred the blood pressure would fall; compensatory changes must occur elsewhere in the system to maintain normal pressure. The brunt of the compensation is borne by the abdominal organs, especially the alimentary canal, and the kidneys. The skin can also be involved but the initial vasoconstriction is often soon overridden when the need to lose heat through the skin becomes paramount. These changes are all coordinated by the vasomotor center in the brain.

The rhythmic breathing pattern appears to be generated within the respiratory center of the brain itself and then modified according to the demands placed on the oxygen supply. Input from

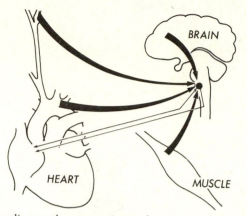

Inputs into the cardiovascular center (curved arrows) which regulate the rate at which the heart beats. The straight arrows represent nerves transmitting this information to the heart.

stretch receptors in the lungs may play a part in limiting inspiration and considerable conscious control can be exerted over breathing. If the carbon dioxide concentration of the blood rises, chemoreceptors in the major blood vessels (aorta and carotid artery) are stimulated and the respiratory rate is increased. The response to a rise in blood carbon dioxide concentration is much more marked than that to a fall in oxygen concentration. But such is the effectiveness of respiratory control that the blood carbon dioxide concentration may actually fall during exercise so that factors other than this must be responsible for feedback control. The most likely mechanisms are an increase in the blood concentration of protons and probably nervous signals produced by the working muscles themselves, in response to local changes in oxygen or carbon dioxide concentration, and transmitted back to the respiratory center.

Although very few studies have been carried out, we would expect training to increase the effectiveness of these control mechanisms. As soon as a change occurs, the body adapts quickly to maintain as near as possible the normal value, whether it is oxygen concentration in the blood or the blood pressure in the major arteries. Ultimately all the changes described in this chapter have evolved to maintain the concentration of ATP in the muscle fibers, and hence permit the enormous increases in energy consumption that are achieved every day by endurance runners during their long hard training sessions.

7

WHAT TRAINING CAN DO FOR YOU

The central part of any training program is regularly repeated exercise, planned not only to perfect techniques but also to stress the various systems that limit performance. It is only by imposing such stresses that capacities are increased. But what systems should be stressed, how frequently and for how long? Often the answer depends upon the coach, the athlete and the current training fashion, but it should be possible to measure and scientifically assess the effects of various training schemes and then select the best. It is reassuring then that the limited number of studies that have been done, often with experimental animals, have tended to justify the training methods arrived at empirically by athletes and their coaches. More studies are needed on human volunteers before we can offer precise advice based on scientific evidence. In this chapter the effects of training will be discussed in relation to the knowledge we have gained from earlier chapters of the biochemistry and physiology of marathon running and sprinting.

Photo on left   Alberto Salazar training in Eugene, Oregon

TRAINING FOR THE MARATHON

Limiting Factors Several processes limit performance in the marathon:

- inhaling oxygen and moving it into the bloodstream
- mobilizing the body's fuel supplies
- controlling the concentration of fuels in the blood
- the volume and rate of flow of blood to the muscles
- the extraction of fuels and oxygen by the muscles
- the rate of ATP synthesis
- controlling the mixture of fuels

We know that all of these processes are affected by training, but the extent to which they are improved and which factor finally limits performance is still debated.

Strengthening the Supply Lines Blood carries oxygen and fuels to the working muscle and waste products away from the muscles. The heart of a trained athlete can pump more blood in less time than the heart of an untrained person. It does so by increasing the stroke volume—the amount of blood expelled by each beat—rather than by increasing the number of beats per minute. Of course, the heart beat increases with exercise, but for the same workload it increases less in the well-trained athlete. The enlarged heart (cardiac hypertrophy) is typical of endurance athletes and is exemplified by the heart of Paavo Nurmi, seven times Olympic champion, which was three times larger than normal.

We might expect that a greater proportion of the blood leaving the heart would flow through the active muscles of a trained runner, but, surprisingly, this is not the case. However, it is true that the runner's cardiovascular system has been improved, not in delivery of more blood to muscles, but in removing oxygen and fuel from the blood flow. At least two factors play a role. The number of capillaries in the muscle increases almost twofold, which very much improves the delivery of oxygen and fuels to each fiber. In addition, the capacities of the metabolic pathways are increased, enabling more oxygen and fuels to be "pulled" into the fibers.

New York City marathon, 1978

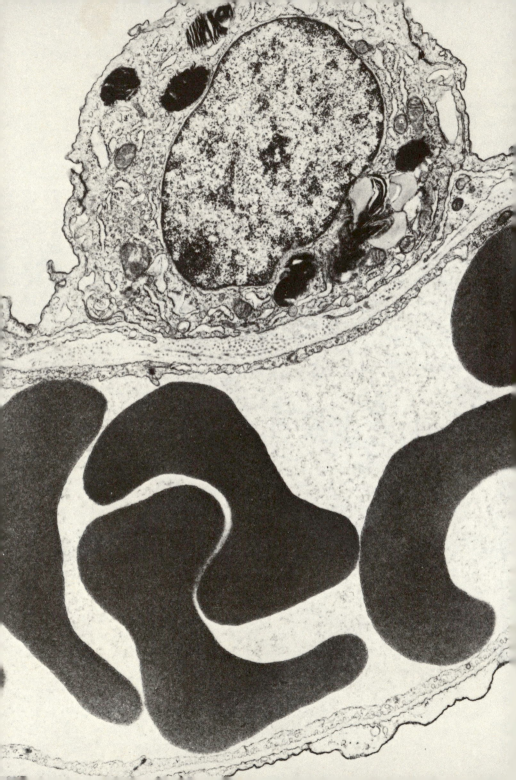

Making More Fuel Available If less of the blood flowing from the heart ends up in the active muscle, where does the remainder go? It ends up in the liver and adipose tissue from which it can carry away the large amounts of mobilized fuels. The transport of fatty acid from adipose tissue to muscle, in elite marathon runners during high power output, may increase almost 80 times that at rest. Good biochemical coordination is required to achieve this increase without, at the same time, raising the blood fatty acid concentration to dangerous levels.

Towards the end of a marathon, when the runner is tired, the liver may convert amino acids to glucose in an attempt to prevent hypoglycemia. This conversion requires ATP, hence the need for a good supply of blood carrying oxygen and fuels. A third tissue which may need to receive extra blood is the skin so that heat can be lost fast enough to prevent hyperthermia.

A Theoretical Speculation

Mobilization of fatty acids is controlled partly by the stress hormones, epinephrine and norepinephrine, the blood concentrations of which rise during running. It comes as something of a shock, therefore, to learn that training actually decreases the levels of these stress hormones. This apparent paradox would be resolved if training increased the sensitivity of fatty-acid mobilization to these stress hormones. To see how this would come about we must look more closely at the process. Triglyceride hydrolysis is catalyzed by a lipase enzyme in the adipose tissue and, once again, the sensitivity of this reaction to control is improved by the operation of a substrate cycle. In this one, the hydrolysis of triglyceride is opposed by reactions in which fatty acids are esterified back to triglyceride. As with the substrate

Red blood cells engaged in oxygen transfer. Air enters through the nose or mouth and passes to the alveoli in the lungs. Within each alveolus oxygen and carbon dioxide diffuse into and out of the bloodstream through the capillaries. In the photo on the left, red blood cells (the large dark and irregularly shaped structures, like figures in a Matisse linolelum cutting) course through a capillary in the lung, taking on oxygen from the air in alveoli.

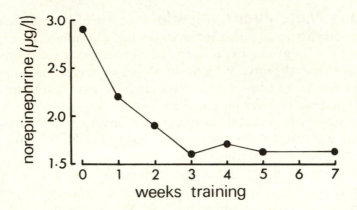

In this experiment, the concentration of norepinephrine in the blood after five minutes of severe exercise was measured at intervals during a seven-week period of intensive training. The level of epinephrine was about one-sixth of this but changed in a similar way.

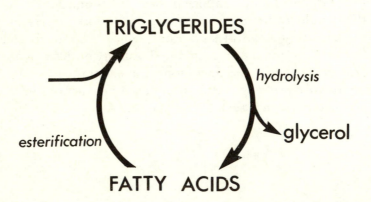

The triglyceride/fatty acid substrate cycle.

cycle in glycolysis, this seemingly wasteful arrangement increases the sensitivity of the pathway to control so that a smaller increase in the levels of the stress hormones in the blood are required to bring about a given increase in the rate of fatty acid mobilization. It is suspected, but it has not yet been proved, that training increases the rate of this substrate cycle.

Changes Within the Fiber No increase in fuel or oxygen supplied to muscles will improve their performance if the fibers are not capable of using the extra supplies. It is especially advantageous for marathon running that training increase the capacity of the fatty acid oxidation system (β-oxidation) in the fiber. This will allow a greater proportion of the ATP generation to arise from fatty acid oxidation, thus conserving precious glycogen reserves and delaying the onset of fatigue. The capacity of the Krebs cycle is also increased.

Although the capacity for anaerobic glycolysis declines in the muscles of a trained endurance runner, the activity of the enzymes that enable glucose to enter the glycolytic pathway actually increases. This reflects an increase in the aerobic metabolism of blood glucose as opposed to the anaerobic metabolism of muscle glycogen.

An intriguing aspect of training is that so many changes occur in an apparently coordinated way. The percentage increase in the capacity for aerobic metabolism is similar to the increase in oxygen supply, brought about by a rise in the number of capillaries. It has even been suggested that muscle fibers possess internal "sensors" which monitor oxygen supply and influence enzyme levels accordingly. One protein that might play a part in such a control is myoglobin. Myoglobin is present only in the muscle fibers and binds oxygen more strongly than does hemoglobin and so "pulls" oxygen into the fibers as it circulates through the capillaries. Training increases the amount of myoglobin in muscle fibers and so increases the rate of diffusion of oxygen.

All these changes occur in both type I and type II fibers, but a marked effect of endurance training is to bring about the conversion of type IIB into type IIA fibers, resulting in a very large change in the total aerobic capacity of the muscle. This change also affects

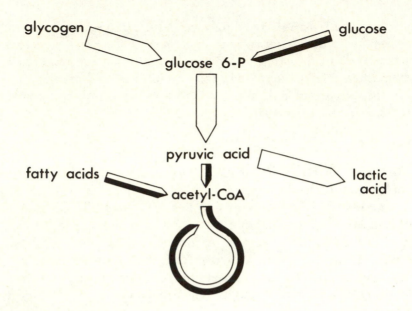

The additional capacity (in black) of metabolic pathways achieved as a result of intensive aerobic training.

the molecular structure of the cross-bridges, which reduces the rate at which cross-bridges cycle. This reduces power output of the muscle but leads to a dramatic increase in endurance.

Interval Versus Distance Training Whether training for the marathon should consist of running long distances without interval training or whether the two should be combined is still debated. Most coaches favor the combined approach and scientific evidence, which is slight, supports their view.

What the marathon runner is trying to do in training is to increase aerobic capacity ($\dot{V}_{O_2 max}$) and the proportion of this that can be sustained for long periods. Just two months training of sedentary individuals can elevate $\dot{V}_{O_2 max}$ by 15–20% and the increase in a year can be 60%. Training also raises the percentage of the $\dot{V}_{O_2 max}$, which can be used for prolonged periods, to 80% or better. It seems likely that these improvements would be best achieved if the runner could train at 100% of the aerobic capacity, since this would stress the aerobic energy-producing systems including the Krebs cycle and β-oxidation. Unfortunately, any attempt to do this for a long period is terminated by fatigue due to lactic acid accumulation as a result of anaerobic glycolysis from glycogen. But short runs of 200–400 meters, separated by short rest periods, remove this problem because any lactic acid formed can be removed by the blood during the rest period. In addition, the small amount of oxygen stored in combination with myoglobin in the fibers is sufficient to maintain largely aerobic metabolism for a short time. Short interval-training of this kind does indeed raise the activity of oxidative capacity of fibers but is probably less effective in improving fuel mobilization and blood supply to tissues. The fact is that in runs of 400 meters or less there is little stress on the mobilization of glucose from liver or fatty acid from adipose tissue. By extending the intervals to a mile, more stress is put on fuel mobilization; for example, 25 g of glycogen can be used in one mile by an elite marathon runner operating at 100% of $\dot{V}O_{2\,max}$. Long interval-training is therefore particularly beneficial when it comes to improving fuel utilization. It also improves the cardiac output. Is there any benefit in longer runs? Certainly there is and most training schedules feature one or two long runs each week. What these runs do is to improve the sensitivity of the mechanisms that coordinate the rates of fuel utilization, especially the relationship between fatty acid and glucose.

The importance of control becomes apparent when you consider what would happen if the rate of fatty acid mobilization exceeded demand by just 1%; in two hours the blood fatty acid concentration would have risen to at least 4 mM, twice the safe level. A number of improvements in metabolic control are apparent from measurements on trained athletes. Little or no lactic acid appears in the blood when the workload on the muscle is increased because of the increased capacity of Krebs cycle and improved coordination between glycolysis and Krebs cycle. A greater proportion of the runner's ATP is generated from fatty acid oxidation due to the increased capacity of β-oxidation and as a result of more effective inhibition of glycolysis by fatty acid oxidation. Long-distance running is probably the best way of stressing these control mechanisms and so providing the body with the stimulus needed to improve their effectiveness.

Altitude Training Living at a high altitude has an effect similar to blood doping. It increases the hematocrit. The atmospheric pressure is lower at higher altitudes and consequently there is less oxygen in each breath. This is a disadvantage for competitors who, residing at sea level, join races at high altitude. Many endurance athletes travelled early to Mexico City for the 1968 Olympic Games, hoping they would adapt to the conditions before the events. But for the elite athlete, the maximum exercise capacity is slightly decreased at high altitude, so the intensity at which the athlete can train is decreased. Consequently, in comparison with the degree of training at sea level, some detraining may occur at altitude, negating the effect of the increased hematocrit. The detraining effect can be overcome by residing at high altitude but travelling every day to sea level for training!

TRAINING FOR THE SPRINT

The factors that limit the performance of sprinters are quite different from those affecting long-distance runners. The anaerobic processes powering the muscle of the sprinter are not dependent on external supplies of fuel or oxygen supply; consequently training does not focus on their management. Instead, the limiting factors are within the fibers or the nerves which control the contraction. Not surprisingly, quite different training techniques are employed. The main elements of sprint-training are regularly repeated short sprints separated by brief recovery periods, weight-training and start-training.

Changing the Very Nature of the Fiber Training for the sprint changes the fiber in at least three ways. During a sprint, ATP is generated from phosphocreatine (in a reaction catalyzed by the enzyme creatine kinase) and from the anaerobic conversion of glycogen to lactic acid. The highest capacities of these two processes are found in type IIB fibers, and strength-training converts type IIA into type IIB fibers. Several changes accompany this transformation: the number of mitochondria is decreased, which allows more space for more myofibrils; the concentration of phosphocreatine, the activity of creatine kinase and the enzymes of glycolysis are increased and the nature of the cross-bridge is changed with an increase in the maximal activity of the cross-bridge ATPase. All of these changes contribute to the increased power output that results from intensive strength-training.

An essential element of the sprint is that power must be developed very rapidly; acceleration is paramount. If glycolysis is to increase to produce sufficient ATP for the myofibrils, the key enzymes must respond very rapidly to changes in ATP and calcium ion concentrations. This would involve an increase in the rate of substrate cycling which is probably a major benefit of start-training.

Strength-training not only causes metabolic changes but also increases fiber thickness by increasing the number of myofibrils per fiber. Since this adds to the number of cross-bridges per fiber, it increases the total activity of cross-bridge ATPase in the muscle and hence its power output. The bulging muscles of the weight-lifter are the outward and visible signs of this increase in the amount of contractile apparatus. The biochemical mechanism by which strength-training causes these changes is not understood but every athlete is aware that other factors, such as diet and drugs, can play a part in increasing muscle mass.

Diet and Drugs The traditional advice to the body-builder, or to anyone intent on increasing the power of their muscles, is to eat large quantities of foods rich in protein (eggs, steak, liver, cheese, milk). On the face of it this is good advice, for any enlargement of the muscle mass must involve additional protein synthesis. Nonetheless, the amount of the increase in muscle protein is small in comparison to the quantity of protein consumed in the diet. If all the protein consumed on a high protein diet was used to increase the amount of skeletal muscle, it should double in less than two months. This is certainly not the case; when the protein content of the diet is increased, much of it is oxidized and the nitrogen excreted as urea. So then is the advice incorrect? Probably it isn't. More likely, our biochemical knowledge is incomplete. Certain amino acids in the dietary protein act as signals to maintain above-average rates of protein synthesis during highly intensive training periods. The very severe strength-training exercises performed by sprinters and other athletes may cause considerable muscle damage each day with a consequent high rate of protein breakdown so, to maintain even normal amounts of muscle protein, high rates of protein synthesis will be necessary. This will require large quantities of building materials, the amino acids, which can only be supplied by protein in the diet.

Special diets have always been considered legitimate means of improving performance, but drugs are another matter. The body-building drugs are the anabolic steroids. Not only is there a problem of unfair competitive advantage—the prizes going to those athletes who have access to the best drugs—but there is a possibility that athletes taking body-building drugs will harm their health. Side effects include sterility, increased incidence of diabetes, coronary heart disease and cancer. Anabolic steroids include the male sex hormone, testosterone, which is responsible for inducing and maintaining the development of the male secondary sexual characteristics. The testes of the average young male secrete about 5 mg of testosterone each day and one function of this hormone is to maintain muscle mass. But to increase muscle mass much larger quantities of testosterone must be ingested, and some athletes are reputed to take 100 times the amount normally secreted each day. Chemically modified forms of testosterone (for example, dianabol) have the advantages that they are not so rapidly degraded by the liver so that smaller quantities are required and, for the female, some of the less welcome side-effects of the male sex hormone are reduced. The disadvantage of the chemically modified forms is that they are readily detected by random urine tests.

Although steroid hormones do increase muscle mass in athletes during training, we don't know how it happens. Some scientists have even suggested that the effect of the drug is primarily on the central nervous system—increasing the feeling of well-being during training sessions so that much harder and longer workouts are possible.

The Importance of Synchrony
If a rowing crew is to achieve maximum exertion, all members of the crew must row. It is the same with muscle; for maximum power all fibers in the muscle must contract. But very seldom do all the fibers contract. It is prevented by a phenomenon called central inhibition. Inhibition

originates in the brain, somehow preventing the locomotory center from stimulating all the nerves to an individual muscle. Clearly this is a safety device. It prevents damage to a muscle, or its antagonistic muscle, which would surely result from the sudden use of excessive force. Part of the strategy of sprint-training is that the runner becomes aware of the available power in a muscle, so that central inhibition can be decreased or removed naturally. With knowledge of a muscle's power the danger of self-inflicted damage is reduced.

Central inhibition can also be decreased by a number of psychological tricks: the shouts, cries or grunts made by a weight-lifter as the big lift is made, or the tennis player as a powerful serve is delivered, may be the conscious or unconscious means of reducing the extent of central inhibition. In times of severe stress, fear or anger, central inhibition may also be removed. Anecdotes of the immense strength exhibited by an otherwise normal mother in rescuing her child may be explained by this phenomenon.

If maximum acceleration from the blocks is to be achieved then not only must all fibers contract, but all must contract simultaneously. Just as a bunch of raw recruits can be "knocked into shape" by a drill sergeant to produce a squad of soldiers that can carry out a drill exercise with the precision of one man, so too can a bunch of muscle fibers be trained to perfect precision. The same conditions apply; a dedicated application to the task by repeated training sessions with the emphasis always on improvement. The perfect control of muscle power, vital to the sprinter, is achieved only by hard training.

SPECIAL TRAINING SITUATIONS

Recovery After Immobilization
Muscle not only develops increased power through use but it becomes weaker and smaller through disuse. The atrophy is well known to anyone who has been confined to bed for a period through illness and is even a problem for astronauts who in the absence of gravity no longer have to maintain muscle tone. It is a particularly serious problem in the athlete who has, for example, a limb immobilized by injury, for muscle wastage in that limb delays return to normal fitness and

competitive standards until well after recovery from the original injury. The cause of this loss of muscle is not known but it involves a gradual loss of myofibrils from the fibers.

Any treatment that maintains some movement or stimulation of muscles in an immobilized person can reduce the extent of wasting. This justifies the current medical practice of giving physiotherapy to patients soon after surgery—even though it may be painful to the patient and distressing to relatives. This treatment maintains the muscles of the patient so that as the damage is repaired, full recovery can occur quickly. Unfortunately, it is not always easy to exercise the muscles; they may, for example, be in a leg that is in plaster. If the leg belongs to a top-class football player, the delay in recovery of the atrophied muscle, once the plaster has been removed, can be financially expensive both for player and club. Research has shown that, if the muscle can be held under tension or if electrical stimulation is applied, the atrophy of the fibers is reduced. Perhaps if we knew the biochemical mechanism by which normal use or electrical stimulation maintained the rates of protein synthesis in muscle, it might be possible to synthesize in the laboratory chemicals that could perform the same function. "Training from a bottle" may still be in the realm of science fiction, but possibly not for much longer.

The Sedentary Non-Runner Very few, if any, studies have been carried out on the effects of training on unfit persons. Those carried out on experimental animals are of questionable relevance if only because a "sedentary" rat (held in a small cage) is probably more physically active than a sedentary executive. The current interest in exercise of all forms, including competitive ball games, keep-fit classes and aerobic dance, can induce the sedentary man or woman to perform well above their aerobic capacity. This could be dangerous if the heart rate and the blood fatty acid concentration increase too dramatically and too quickly. In contrast, running has a built-in feedback control involving pain and discomfort not so easily dismissed by those who succumb to the competitive urge of the ball game or the rhythm of the dance music. Mild endurance training (jogging) can slowly but surely improve oxidative capacity, and incidentally decrease the dangers inherent in such activities as competitive ball games and aerobic dance. We recommend that some jogging be done by squash players, participants in aerobic dance and keep-fit classes.

Serious and committed endurance training can produce truly dramatic results. Many of those competing in the first London marathon (March 1981) had done no more than six months carefully planned training and had never run seriously before. Of the 7,000 who started the run, 6,255 finished within 5 hours.

Getting Started

1   Walk increasingly greater distances up to several miles.

2   Jog gently for 100 yards; walk for 300 yards and repeat for increasing distances.

3   Jog for 1 mile, gradually extending the distance.

Two criteria of exertion have been recommended to protect the unfit person from harmful physiological stress during these early stages. The first is that it should always be possible to carry on a conversation while jogging. Secondly, the heart rate should never exceed 180 minus the age of the runner . . . you will be amazed at your progress and improvement.

8

HEALTH AND THE RUNNER

There is no doubt that running is physiologically traumatic and consequently is not without its dangers; but then this is true for any sport. What we have tried to do is to assess the scientific evidence for both the benefits and dangers, to explain them in relation to the knowledge gained from earlier chapters and to show how that metabolic knowledge can enhance these benefits and minimize the dangers. Although we have attempted to carry out this assessment objectively, we do not feel that it precludes us from holding the opinion that, on balance, running greatly benefits both body and mind.

MUSCLE DAMAGE: A PROBLEM OR THE ELIXIR OF LIFE?

The Problem There is no doubt that damage is caused to muscles as a result of prolonged running. Ask any marathon runner for the symptoms and the reply will be: weakness, stiffness, pain on moving and cramps. The physiological, biochemical or structural basis for these problems is far from clear but the knowledge gained from earlier chapters helps us to make some suggestions. The

Photo on left   Bonnie Belle Race

Penny Hall, who made such a remarkable recovery from serious illness by becoming a runner, shown here in the warrior pose.

weakness and pain on moving are probably directly related to the depletion of glycogen within the muscle. When movement begins, the fibers are unable to generate ATP at the rate required by the cross-bridge cycling and the ATP concentration falls. The decrease in the ATP concentration leads immediately to the symptoms of fatigue, including stimulation of pain receptors.

Damage to the blood capillaries within the muscle may compound the problem by preventing ATP generation from the Krebs cycle. This increases the dependence on anaerobic glycolysis and muscle glycogen. Capillary damage may also cause abnormal ion gradients in the muscle leading to cramps, a common enough complaint although its biochemical basis is not yet understood.

Biopsy samples taken from muscles after severe sustained exercise have revealed damage to the myofibrils themselves, particularly to the Z-lines. Indeed, the damage is great enough to explain why tenderness and pain may persist for up to three weeks. During this time, cellular repairs begin by breaking down damaged structures and making replacement parts. The muscle then needs an increased supply of fuels, oxygen, building materials and white blood cells (to consume the debris), which are made quickly available by an increase in the permeability of blood vessels in the damaged tissue. This increased permeability is brought about by chemical agents, called prostaglandins, released by the damaged fibers. These prostaglandins also increase the sensitivity of local pain receptors so that the whole area becomes painful to move or touch. In fact, the pain is a means of protecting the damaged tissue from activities which would disturb and hinder the delicate repair processes. If evidence is needed that all is not known about damage and repair of muscle during running you only have to look at some of the spectacular repetitive running feats that have been achieved, such as that by Frank Giannino who in 1980 ran 4,989 kilometers in just over 46 days, an average of two and a half marathons each day. Either little or no damage was caused each day or repair was remarkably rapid.

There is evidence that tissues other than muscle are damaged by running, including liver, kidney and even the brain. It is unclear why this should be, unless the massive demand for blood by the active muscles reduces the supply to other tissues; causing a deficiency of oxygen and so damage to some cells.

The Elixir Since it is a tenet of modern society that pain and discomfort be reduced to a minimum, the runner receives little sympathy from friends and colleagues when recovering from a race. They may even question the runner's sanity but what the critics do not realize is that this self-inflicted damage may be of real benefit.

Our bodies are nothing if not adaptable and it is almost invariably the case that increased use of a function leads to an increase in its capacity. In this instance, not only does regular exercise improve the capacity of repair processes, but also of the complex and carefully controlled degradative processes which remove damaged cell constituents. The cycle of degradation and replacement of cell constituents, known as turnover, occurs continuously in every tissue—even when it is not damaged. Turnover prevents the build-up of proteins that can no longer carry out their normal function, and replaces them with normally functioning proteins. It is equivalent to having one's automobile serviced every day. However, there is evidence that these turnover processes become less effective with age and indeed ageing may be a consequence of the accumulation of non-functional proteins in a cell.

All this indicates that, far from being harmful, the tissue damage that results from severe exercise may actually slow down the ageing process by "purging" muscle and other tissues (including heart, lung, liver and brain) of abnormal and potentially dangerous proteins. Could some of the worse effects of ageing, such as physical immobility and senile dementia, be delayed or prevented by regular exercise?

CARDIOVASCULAR BENEFITS

Cardiovascular disease kills over three-quarters of a million Americans each year. But the interesting fact is that since the 1970s this number is falling. Is it just a coincidence that this fall comes at a time when the popularity of running is so high?

Heart Attacks The classic heart attack is the final event in a long series of changes which probably occur to some extent in everyone. The attack can be accelerated by a variety of predispos-

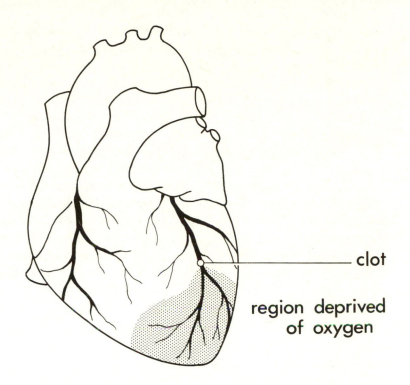

clot

region deprived
of oxygen

The consequence of a blood clot in a coronary artery.

ing factors: stress, obesity, lack of exercise, high-cholesterol diets, high blood pressure, being male and tobacco smoking. The immediate pathological cause is the failure of part of the cardiac muscle to get an adequate supply of oxygen because one of the coronary arteries, or a branch of the artery, has become blocked by a blood clot. The chances of a clot forming and of becoming lodged in the coronary arteries is enormously increased by a condition known as atherosclerosis, which is the deposition of fatty and fibrous material in the arterial wall, reducing the internal diameter of the artery. In order to understand how running might decrease the rate at which atherosclerosis develops, we must first examine its origins.

The arteries, through which blood travels to all tissues of the body, are not simple tubes but have walls composed of three layers. The outer layer is tough but elastic, accommodating changes in diameter brought about by the smooth muscle cells in the middle layer. The innermost layer is much thinner and composed of endothelial cells forming a barrier between the blood and the smooth muscle cells. These endothelial cells appear prone to damage by factors which include high blood pressure, tobacco smoking and high levels of blood fatty acids. This damage increases the permeability of the endothelial cells so that the smooth muscle cells come into contact with the constituents of the blood. One of these constituents, the platelets, release chemicals which cause the smooth muscle fibers to multiply and so thicken the wall. In addition, fat-containing particles, especially the low-density lipoproteins (known as LDL), gain access to and are taken up by the smooth muscle fibers. These particles contain appreciable amounts of cholesterol which accumulates in the muscle fibers causing some of them to die. In turn, fiber death stimulates other

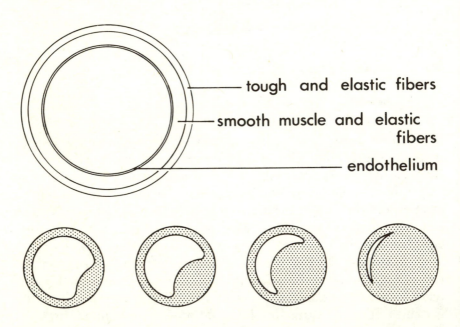

tough and elastic fibers

smooth muscle and elastic fibers

endothelium

The cross-section through a major artery shows the layered structure of its wall. Atherosclerosis leads to a progressive occlusion of arteries, as shown in the lower sequence.

How a heart attack comes about and how it might be prevented.

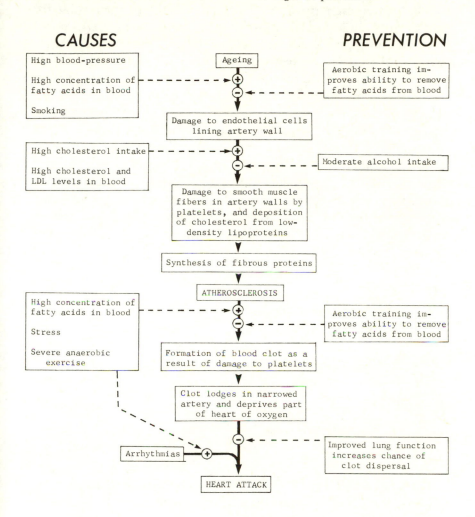

CAUSES   PREVENTION

cells in the layer to produce a fibrous protein, similar to collagen, which further thickens the wall and intrudes into the lumen of the artery, so reducing its diameter. Atherosclerosis is the result.

    Although this simplified account casts cholesterol in the role of villain, cholesterol is, in fact, an essential constituent of all cell membranes. It also assists in the transport of triglyceride in the blood. But when there is too much cholesterol there is a problem.

There is a further dimension to the cholesterol story. There are two fat-containing particles in the blood which are responsible for transporting cholesterol, the low-density lipoprotein (LDL) particles and the high-density lipoprotein (HDL) particles. HDL removes cholesterol from the tissues and transfers it into other particles in the blood. LDL, on the other hand, obtains its cholesterol from these other particles and transfers it to the tissues. This implies that HDL-cholesterol is "safer" than LDL-cholesterol and studies do show an inverse relationship between a high HDL-cholesterol/LDL-cholesterol ratio and coronary heart disease. Running, especially marathon running, has been shown to raise this ratio in men. This finding could explain how physical activity protects against the heart attack. It may be of interest to some readers to know that a moderate consumption of alcohol increases the HDL-cholesterol/LDL-cholesterol ratio and so also reduces the incidence of heart disease.

TABLE 8.1 CHOLESTEROL

Persons	PLASMA CHOLESTEROL CONCENTRATIONS (MILLIGRAMS PER 100 ml)		
	Total Cholesterol	LDL Cholesterol	HDL Cholesterol
Inactive subjects	211.7	136.5	43.3
Joggers	204.2	125.0	58.0
Marathon runners	187.2	107.0	64.8

Cholesterol is found in lipoproteins other than HDL and LDL.

Sudden Death During Exercise Reports of deaths occurring either during or immediately after strenuous exercise are seized upon by those anxious to prove that exercise does much more harm than good. A South African study indicated that such deaths were more likely to occur in competitive ball games such as rugby, soccer or squash rather than running. We believe that some of the deaths could have had a metabolic basis and, if this is the case, it suggests how running could provide protection from the heart attack. During exercise, the concentrations of the stress hormones, epinephrine and norepinephrine, rise and these stimulate the release of fatty acid from stored triglyceride. This provides fuel

TABLE 8.2   SUDDEN DEATH

Type of Sport	Number of Deaths	Average Age at Time of Death
Rugby football	7	26
Soccer	2	43
Golf	1	40
Mountaineering	1	47
Tennis	2	54
Jogging	1	46
Yachting	1	38

Details were collected during an 18 month period in South Africa.

for the muscles during exercise and is a perfectly normal and safe process. Unfortunately, problems can arise if the concentration of fatty acids exceeds that which can be transported in combination with the carrier protein albumin, about 2 mM. If this happens, the concentration of *free* fatty acids increases not only in the bloodstream but also within many of the cells of the body and this can result in damage to cell membranes, initiation of blood clots due to platelet adhesion, and interference with electrical transmission across the heart. All of these are dangerous and either of the latter two effects could cause heart failure and death.

Fatty acids are used as a fuel for muscle primarily during sustained exercise, but most ball games involve short sharp explosive bursts of activity for which energy is obtained from phosphocreatine and from the conversion of glycogen to lactic acid. Hence fatty acids are not used rapidly. If the control mechanisms are not sufficiently precise, fatty acids accumulate and exceed the safe capacity of the blood. The stress of competition (manifested as aggression towards the opposition) further increases the concentrations of circulating stress hormones and this can only make matters worse. It follows from all this that those undertaking aerobic exercise (such as jogging, cycling, swimming, rowing) are in a much better position because the rate of fatty acid utilization is greater and this type of exercise 'trains' the precision of the complex mechanism of control of fatty acid mobilization.

Problems caused by high levels of fatty acids in the blood are not restricted to those participating in sports. In primitive man and in animals in the wild it is easy to see the benefits of increased fuel

TABLE 8.3 FATTY ACIDS

Fatty Acids in the Blood	Fatty Acid Concentration (mMolar)
Normally fed men	0.30–0.60
Stress (racing driver)	1.72
Starvation (8 days—Harvard divinity students)	1.88
Prolonged exercise (240 minutes—Stockholm firemen)	1.83
Ultra-distance runners after completion of 100 km (63 mile) run	1.90
Patients in diabetic coma (blood taken as soon as patients enter emergency room)	1.60
Severely burned patients	1.30

There is usually considerable variation in the concentrations of fatty acids in normally fed subjects; this probably reflects the degree of anxiety in the subject when a blood sample is taken. Despite severity of conditions, the concentrations of fatty acid do not exceed 2 mM indicating the precision of the control of fatty acid mobilization.

mobilization under stressful circumstances, the most likely responses to stress being "fight or flight". But in modern man, who has evolved socially far faster than he has biologically, stress-inducing situations are usually very different. These may include driving through heavy traffic, conflict at work or at home, losing a job or getting a divorce. The important point is that although all of these can raise the blood fatty acid concentration, none are followed by exercise which will consume the fuel.

One of the greatest benefits of regular aerobic exercise may be to increase the capacity of muscles to use fatty acids as a fuel and so reduce the time their concentration remains elevated, even when there is no opportunity for exercise. Nonetheless, we would advise someone who anticipates exposure to a stressful situation to delay their daily run until after the stress. Any excess fatty acids will soon be oxidized out of harm's way.

STRESS, FATTY ACIDS AND A PLANE CRASH

Although there are a number of reports of pilots being incapacitated by a heart attack, perhaps the best known is the crash of the British European Airways Trident soon after take-off on June 18th, 1972. A post mortem on the pilot, Captain Key, showed severe atherosclerosis in the coronary arteries and evidence of a previous minor infarction. Despite this, as the official report states, "Captain Key presented to those who knew him a picture of robust good health," and he was passed fit to fly by a medical examination in November, 1971. Of particular relevance to the present discussion is that one and a half hours before take-off Captain Key had been involved in an altercation in the crew room over whether pilots should take strike action in support of a claim for higher salaries. Captain Key was directly involved in a heated argument and he was reported to be very angry indeed. We suggest that the disagreement was a stress condition which may have lasted for most of the period prior to take-off and would have been extended by the pre-flight preparation and the take-off itself. The official report concludes that Captain Key had a heart attack during take-off and that consequently he suffered pain and malaise which would have impaired his judgment and his mental faculties. Thus the aircraft failed to maintain sufficient speed and the droops (retractable leading-edge high-lift devices) were retracted too early during the take-off. This produced a stall and resulted in the crash. Did the stress of the pre-flight argument contribute to the heart attack by raising the fatty acid concentration above the safe limit of 2 mM? If Captain Key had been a keen runner would the accident have occurred?

EXCEEDING THE LIMITS

Although, as we have tried to show above, many of the alleged dangers of running have been overstated, some are very real. The short list of life-threateners, which the marathon runner in particular must learn to recognize and avoid, includes extremes of body-temperature, dehydration and a catastrophic fall in blood glucose concentration.

Overheating The runner expends a considerable amount of chemical energy almost all of which appears as heat. On a cold day, heat obtained from exercise is important in helping to maintain the body temperature which is close to 98.4°F (37°C). During

The remedy for overheating in Sri Lanka

a marathon the rate of heat production can be more than 1 kW or at least thirteen times greater than that at rest. A major problem facing the marathon runner is to achieve adequate heat loss in order to prevent hyperthermia, that is, an elevated body temperature. (The prefix hyper- means above, hypo- means below, so that hypothermia is a body temperature below normal.) Hyperthermia can lead to heat stroke in which the mechanisms maintaining body temperature no longer operate. It is characterized by irritability, aggressive behavior, disorientation, unsteady gait and a glassy stare. In the Empire Games in Canada in 1954, heat stroke caused the British runner Jim Peters to collapse in the final 400 meters of the marathon; a British cyclist, Tony Simpson, suffered fatal heat stroke in the Tour de France in 1959, and Alberto Salazar was sufficiently near death, from heat stroke in August 1978 after the

Falmouth, Mass. road race, to be administered the last rites.

To prevent hyperthermia, heat produced in the muscles must be lost from the body, and this means transporting the heat from the core of the body to its surface—the skin. By increasing the flow of blood through the skin heat is lost from the body. Heat is lost, not only by convection and conduction, but also as a result of evaporation of water from the skin. Several liters of sweat may be produced during a marathon, playing a vital part in the cooling process.

Heatstroke is most likely to occur on a hot humid day. The air is then unable to hold much more water vapor, so that little evaporation can occur. But runners are so keen to run that races take place even in such conditions. What precautions should be taken? Fluid should be taken before and during the race; splash the body with water at every feeding station. Soak your headband and T-shirt, if you wear them, for evaporation from these surfaces will carry away considerable heat.

The problem of hyperthermia is compounded by dehydration. Unfortunately, the sensation of thirst cannot be relied upon to detect dehydration, and once it has set in matters go from bad to worse. To detect hyperthermia, feel the skin at the top of the chest—if it has become warm and dry the runner should slow and obtain liquid as soon as possible. Unfortunately this test is not always reliable and runners who feel unwell for a period of time on hot, humid days should stop and take medical advice.

Underheating and Hypoglycemia
Low blood sugar concentration is called hypoglycemia. Blood glucose, as we saw in Chapter 4, is replenished by the breakdown of glycogen in the liver. Unfortunately, liver glycogen is soon exhausted; and despite sophisticated control mechanisms, large demands for energy can seriously decrease the blood glucose concentration. The reason this is so serious is that blood glucose keeps the brain alive; when the blood concentration is decreased by 50% or more, the life of the brain is in danger. Nausea, weakness, sweating, palpitations, a feeling of detachment from the environment, visual disturbances and fine tremor are the symptoms. Hypoglycemia can occur after the race, when the runner is relaxing, as well as during the race.

Fortunately, ingestion of glucose—preferably in a dilute solution (5 gram per 100 ml) provides a quick cure.

In the 1982 Boston marathon, Alberto Salazar and Dick Beardsley battled out the last 10 miles and Salazar won in the record time of 2 hours 8 minutes and 51 seconds, only two seconds ahead of Beardsley. However, Salazar collapsed after the race and needed medical treatment. Although dehydrated, he appeared to be suffering from hypothermia rather than hyperthermia, which may have been related to severe hypoglycemia, probably caused by the enormous effort required to win the race. The combination of hypoglycemia and hypothermia clearly can be dangerous. Salazar recovered after intravenous infusion of a glucose solution. This suggests that even elite runners can run out of all their glycogen reserves.

Regular aerobic exercise not only leads to a greater rate of glucose utilization but it also increases the sensitivity of muscle to insulin—it combats the effect of ageing! In normal sedentary man the concentration of blood glucose is controlled, in part, by secretion of insulin by the pancreas. This hormone increases glucose utilization by muscle. As we get older, muscle becomes less sensitive to this effect of insulin, and the blood glucose concentration rises to higher levels after meals. These higher levels favor a reaction between glucose and proteins which leads to damage of capillary walls with the eventual possibility of decreasing blood flow. The problem of increasing glucose utilization is particularly important in diabetic patients for whom exercise is strongly recommended.

WEIGHT CONTROL AND RUNNING

The cause of obesity is straightforward. More chemical energy is ingested than is oxidized. The extra energy is used to synthesize triglycerides, which are stored in adipose tissue. In non-obese people, the so-called appetite-satiety center in the brain somehow senses the amount of adipose tissue in the body and adjusts both food intake and energy expenditure accordingly. Losing weight is so difficult for some people because they are unable to raise their energy expenditure sufficiently to avoid triglyceride deposition on

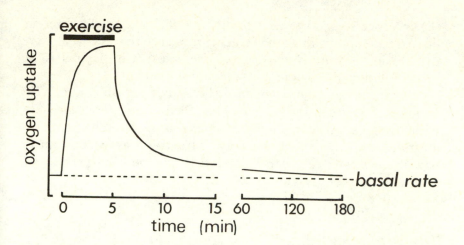

Additional oxygen uptake persists for a very long time after vigorous exercise (perhaps for 24 hours). Note the change of timescale of this 'recovery oxygen' uptake.

even a very moderate diet.

One way of increasing energy expenditure would be to use your muscles more, converting chemical energy into movement and ultimately heat, but the ideal candidate for energy-shedding is a process which achieves nothing except the conversion of chemical energy to heat energy. This is virtually the definition of a substrate cycle, such as that described in Chapter 5 in which the enzymes phosphofructokinase and fructose bisphosphatase are simultaneously active so that the overall reaction is the hydrolysis of ATP. Calculations show that operation of this cycle, together with others like it, could easily dissipate enough energy to play a useful role in weight regulation.

Substrate cycles may well provide the answer to another metabolic mystery and in so doing provide a link between running and weight control. It is well known that after periods of anaerobic exercise there is an oxygen consumption in excess of what is apparently needed at that time. This has become known as the "oxygen debt" but is more rationally termed "recovery oxygen". Several processes undoubtedly contribute to this extra consumption including substrate cycles which are involved in the regulation of repair processes and the restoration of fuel stores. Two recent discoveries support this involvement; these are that recovery oxygen is also a feature of aerobic exercise and that it may persist at least 24 hours after endurance exercise is over.

Regular exercise will enhance the activity of substrate cycle enzymes. As a result the body will be able to deal more effectively with any chemical energy ingested in excess of immediate requirements or normal storage capacity. This confirms what runners have been saying for years in the face of doubts expressed by nutritional experts.

The Woman Runner

Of the 30,000,000 people in the U.S.A. said to run or jog regularly, 30% or more are women. Virtually everything to be found elsewhere in this book applies equally to both sexes. But women are different in that they alone have the ability to bear children and nourish them both before and after birth. How does this affect a woman's running? Probably not at all unless she is actually pregnant and then the difficulty will be obvious enough. But running may affect her reproductive life. Women runners are prone to disturbances of their menstrual cycles, which may fail to occur entirely, a condition known as amenorrhea. There is indeed a correlation between the number of miles run per week and the incidence of this condition.

Women naturally possess around twice as much stored triglyceride as men. This difference is characteristic of most other mammals too and reflects the greatly increased fuel requirements during pregnancy and especially lactation; as much as 50% above normal. If the proportion of body fat in a woman falls much below about 25% of her body weight, menstrual cycles tend to become irregular and may cease altogether. This results in temporary infertility and provides a sound biological means of contraception to avoid the real danger of child-bearing without the reserves necessary to nurse the baby. The problem for the non-obese runner is that her increased rate of fat utilization may reduce her proportion of adipose tissue below the critical level. To counteract this effect, the runner must increase her energy intake to increase her fat deposits. In practice, this is best achieved by eating more carbohydrate (for example bread, potatoes, pasta and cereals) since a high-fat diet can bring other problems. By carefully following her body weight and making the appropriate dietary adjustments the female runner should be able to avoid menstrual imbalance.

Women can suffer from painful and prolonged menstruation, a condition known as dysmenorrhea. Anecdotal evidence suggests that running can enormously improve this condition.

THE RUNNING "HIGH"

Although aware of the long-term health benefits, most runners claim that they run because it makes them feel good. There is much anecdotal evidence in favor of these claims—one of the first was related by Siegfried Sassoon in his *Memoirs of an Infantry Officer*, published in 1930, in which he describes the difficulties of life in the trenches during World War I:

> "Of course there is a hell of a lot of physical discomfort to be put up with, and the unpleasant sights seem to get worse every year; but, apart from being shelled and so on, I must say I've often felt extraordinarily happy, even in the trenches . . . it's probably something to do with being in the open air so much and getting such a lot of exercise".

A Chemical Explanation: Neurotransmitters It is widely accepted that at least some aspects of mood are determined by the concentrations of neurotransmitters in the brain. Neurotransmitters, sometimes called chemical messengers, convey information from one nerve to another, allowing the completion of nervous circuits upon which all our actions and experiences depend. We know that some antidepressant drugs act by increasing the concentration of a group of neurotransmitters called the monoamines. Exercise may have exactly the same effect. In fact, studies suggest that exercise does improve mood in some depressed patients.

Exercise might increase the concentration of neurotransmitters in the brain indirectly, via a group of substances called amino acids. Twenty kinds of amino acids provide the building blocks from which all proteins, including enzymes and the structural proteins of muscle, are made. In addition, some amino acids have

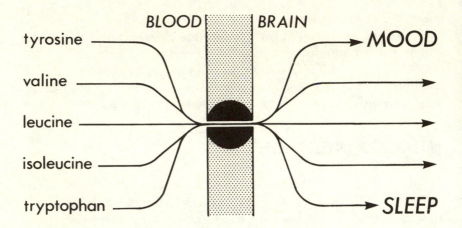

Competition between amino acids for a single type of carrier to transport them from the blood into brain cells. Exercise might lower the blood concentrations of valine, leucine and isoleucine since these amino acids are oxidised by muscle. Consequently, the competition for the entry of tyrosine and tryptophan into the brain will be decreased, and more of these amino acids in the brain will result in a faster rate of manufacture and hence in higher concentrations of neurotransmitters and behavioral effects as indicated.

special roles in the body, and two of these roles interact in an intriguing way that relates exercise to brain function. The amino acids tyrosine and tryptophan serve as starting points for the manufacture of the monoamine neurotransmitters which include norepinephrine, 5-hydroxytryptamine and dopamine. The manufacture of the monoamines is increased as a direct result of strenuous exercise, and we may suppose their concentration in the brain increases too. In this way, an improvement in mood would come about.

It is not difficult to see how the link between exercise and mood could have evolved considering the important part played by physical activity in the life of man. The reward of an improved mood, a feeling of well-being after exercise, would provide a natural incentive for regular exercise. This would ensure that muscles were maintained in good condition, so enhancing the chances of successful breeding, and the propagation of the genes which determine the characteristics.

Endorphins Of the large number of compounds with neurotransmitter activity which have been found in the brain recently, a particularly interesting group are the endorphins. These are a group of peptides or mini-proteins which may control the response of neurons receiving sensory information from pain receptors, including pain receptors in muscle stimulated by fatigue. Endorphins seem to reduce the effect of sensory impulses from such pain receptors and so can eliminate, or dull, pain. In fact, it seems very likely that one of the best pain killing drugs, known as morphine, acts by mimicking the effect of naturally produced endorphins in the brain. Perhaps runners who are able to run amazingly long distances, such as marathoners, can do so because their brain responds by increasing the concentration of endorphins, and so dulling the sensation of pain. It is tempting to find a parallel between the addictive properties of morphine and the addiction shown by many to their daily run.

HEALTH AWARENESS

Runners spend a lot of time thinking about their bodies, and how to maintain peak efficiency. The need for an effective oxygen supply to the muscles, for example, will be much clearer to the runner than the non-runner, in whom the consequences of a poor supply will be less apparent. The runner who contemplates a marathon cannot tolerate 10% of the hemoglobin being inactivated by combination with carbon monoxide, so the runner gives up smoking. Furthermore, from regular training runs-especially when building up for a long race such as a marathon—it will be clear that too much alcohol, too little sleep and the wrong diet interferes with the running. In other words, the commitment to running introduces a wider concern for health and well-being. Fit runners can accurately assess their own health because of the knowledge they have gained about their body; they know how to treat the body to maintain it in top class condition and have an early warning system when something goes wrong. This is probably the greatest health benefit of running.

ILLUSTRATION ACKNOWLEDGEMENTS

Cover, Janeart, Ltd.
Facing page 1, Steven Sutton, Duomo
Page 14, micrograph by Mrs. Barbara Luke
Page 16, Michael Grimaldi, Duomo
Page 21, micrograph by Professor Brenda Ryman
Page 33, Mrs. Hans Krebs
Page 36, Steven Sutton, Duomo
Page 38, Mark Shearman
Page 40, micrograph by Dr. David Smith
Page 46, Dr. C. A. Maunder-Sewry and V. Dubowitz
Page 48, Steven Sutton, Duomo
Page 59, Mark Shearman
Page 68, Steven Sutton, Duomo
Page 73, Steven Sutton, Duomo
Page 80, Donald Getsug, Photo Researchers, Inc.
Page 94, Steven Sutton, Duomo
Page 108, Steven Sutton, Duomo
Page 111, Jan Lukas, Photo Researchers, Inc.
Page 112, E. R. Weibel
Page 124, Gale Constable, Duomo
Page 126, Mark Shearman
Page 136, G. Daniell, Photo Researchers, Inc.

REFERENCES

Chapter 1

Åstrand, P. O. & Rodahl, K. 1977. *Textbook of physiology. Physiologic basis of exercise.* 2nd Edit. New York: McGraw-Hill Book Co.

Wilmore, J. H. 1983. Body composition in sport and exercise: directions for future research. *Med. Sci. Sports Exercise, 15:* 21–31.

Chapter 2

Crabtree, B. & Taylor, B. J. 1979. Thermodynamics and metabolism. In *Biochemical Thermodynamics* (Ed. Jones, N. M.) Amsterdam: Elsevier, pp. 333–378.

Durnin, J. G. V. A. & Passmore, R. 1967. *Energy, Work and Leisure.* London: Heinemann.

Margaria, R. 1976. *Biomechanics and Energetics of Muscular Exercise.* Oxford: Clarendon Press.

Newsholme, E. A. & Leech, A. R. 1983. *Biochemistry for the Medical Sciences.* Chichester, U.K.: John Wiley & Sons Ltd.

Alexander, R. McN. 1977. Terrestrial locomotion. In *Mechanics and Energetics of Animal Locomotion* (eds. Alexander, R. McN. & Goldspink, G.) London: Chapman & Hall, pp. 118–203.

Chapter 3

White, D. C. S. 1977. Muscle mechanics. In *Mechanics and Energetics of Animal Locomotion* (eds. Alexander, R. McN. & Goldspink, G.) London: Chapman & Hall pp. 23–56.

Wilkie, D. 1976. *Muscle.* London: E. Arnold.

Chapter 4

Costill, D. L. & Fox, E. L. 1969. Energetics of marathon running. *Med. Sci. Sports Exercise, 1:* 81–86.

Costill, D. L., Coyle, E. & Dalsky, G. 1977. Effects of elevated plasma FFA and insulin on muscle glycogen usage during exercise. *J. Appl. Physiol. 43:* 695–699.

Costill, D. L. & Miller, J. M. 1980. Nutrition for endurance sport: carbohydrate and fluid balance. *Int. J. Sports Medicine, 1:* 2–14.

Davies, C. T. M. & Thompson, M. W. 1979. Aerobic performance of female marathon and male ultramarathon athletes. *Eur. J. Appl. Physiol. 41:* 233–245.

Hall, G. M., Lucke, J. N., Masheter, K. *et al.* 1981. Metabolic and hormonal changes during prolonged exercise in the horse. In *Biochemistry of Exercise,* IV.A (Ed. Poortmans, J. & Niset, G.) Baltimore: University Park Press, pp. 88–92.

Chapter 5

Asmussen, E., 1979. Muscle fatigue. *Med. Sci. Sports Exercise, 11:* 313–321.

Costill, D. L., Daniels, J., Evans, W. *et al.* (1976). Skeletal muscle enzymes and fiber composition in male and female track athletes. *J. Appl. Physiol. 40:* 149–154.

Edwards, R. H. T. 1981. Human muscle function and fatigue. *Ciba Found. Symp. 82:* 1–18.

Hermansen, L. 1981. Effect of metabolic changes on force generation in skeletal muscle during maximal exercise. *Ciba Found. Symp. 8:* 75–88.

Snow, D. H. & Guy, P. S. 1980. Muscle fiber type composition of a number of limb muscles in different types of horse. *Res. Vet. Sci. 28:* 137–144.

Chapter 6

Costill, D. L. 1979. A Scientific Approach to Distance Running. Los Altos, California: Track & Field News.

Hagan, R. D., Smith, M. G. & Gettman, L. R. 1981. Marathon performance in relation to maximal aerobic power and training induced. *Med. Sci.* Sports Exercise, *13:* 185–189.

Chapter 7

Baldwin, K. M., Winder, W. W., Terjung, R. L. *et al.* 1973. Glycolytic enzymes in different types of skeletal muscle: adaptation to exercise. *Am. J. Physiol. 225:* 962–966.

Buick, F. J., Gledhill, N., Froese, A. B. *et al.* 1980. Effect of induced erythrocythemia on aerobic work capacity. *J. Appl. Physiol. 48:* 636–642.

Eriksson, E. 1981. Rehabilitation of muscle function after sport injury—major problem in sports medicine. *Int. J. Sports Medicine, 2:* 1–6.

Freed, D. L. J. & Banks, A. J. 1975. A double-blind cross-over trial of methanedienone ('Dianabol') in moderate dosage on highly trained experienced athletes. *Brit. J. Sports Medicine, 9:* 78–81.

Galbo, H. 1983. *Hormonal and metabolic adaptation to exercise.* Stuttgart & New York: George Thieme Verlag.

Howald, H. 1982. Training-induced morphological and functional changes in skeletal muscle. *Int. J. Sports Medicine, 3:* 1–12.

Lydiard, A. 1978. *Run the Lydiard Way.* London: Hodder.

Sargeant, A. J., Davies, C. T. M., Edwards, R. A. T. *et al.* 1977. Functional and structural changes after disuse of human muscle. *Clin. Sci. Mol. Med. 52:* 337–342.

Shepard, R. J. 1978. *The Fit Athlete.* Oxford: Oxford University Press.

Wilt, F. 1964. *Run, run, run.* Los Altos, California: Track & Field News Inc.

Chapter 8

Decombaz, J., Reinhardt, P., Anantharaman, K. *et al.* 1979. Biological changes in a 100 km run: free amino acids, urea and creatinine. *Eur. J. Appl. Physiol. 41:* 61–72.

Folkins, C. H. & Sime, W. E. 1981. Physical fitness training and mental health. *Am. Psychol. 36:* 373–389.

Frisch, R. E., Wyshak, G. & Vincent, L. 1980. Delayed menarche and amenorrhea in ballet dancers. *New Engl. J. Med. 303:* 17–19.

Hartung, G. H., Foreyt, J. P., Mitchell, R. E. *et al.* 1980. Relationship of diet to high-density-lipoprotein cholesterol in middle-aged marathon runners, joggers and inactive men. *New Engl. J. Med. 302:* 357–361.

Holloszy, J. O. 1983. Exercise, health and ageing: a need for more information. *Med. Sci. Sports Exercise,* 15:1–5.

Lancet editorial 1982. Running, jumping and amenorrhea. *Lancet ii:* 638–640.

Lees, R. S. & Lees, A. M. 1982. High density lipoproteins and risk of atherosclerosis. *New Engl. J. Med. 306:* 1546–1548.

Lemon, P. W. R. & Nagle, F. J. 1981. Effects of exercise on protein and amino acid metabolism. *Med. Sci. Sports Exercise, 13:* 141–149.

Milvy, P. & Siegel, A. J. 1981. Physical activity levels and altered mortality from coronary heart disease with an emphasis on marathon running: a critical review. *Cardiovasc. Rev. Rep. 2:* 233–236.

Morgan, W. P. 1980. The trait psychology controversy. *Res. Quart. Exercise Sport, 51:* 50–76.

Morris, J. N., Everitt, M. G., Pollard, R. *et al.* 1980. Vigorous exercise in leisure time: protection against coronary heart disease. *Lancet ii:* 1207–1210.

Opie, L. H. 1975. Sudden death and sport. *Lancet i:* 263–266.

Paffenbarger, R. S. & Hyde, R. T. 1980. Exercise as protection against heart attacks. *New Engl. J. Med. 302:* 1026–1027.

Rennie, M. J., Edwards, R. H. T., Davies, C. T. M. 1980. Protein and amino acid turnover during and after exercise. *Biochemical Society Transactions, 8:* 499–501.

Taggart, P. & Carruthers, M. 1971. Endogenous hyperlipidemia induced by emotional stress of racing drivers. *Lancet i:* 363–366.

Thompson, P. D., Funk, E. J., Carleton, R. A. *et al.* 1982. Incidence of death during jogging in Thode Island from 1975 through 1980. *J. Am. Med. Ass.* 247: 2535–2538.

Tunstall-Pedoe, D. 1979. Exercise and sudden death. *Brit. J. Sports Medicine, 12:* 215–219.

Willet, W., Hennekers, C. H., Siegel, A. T. *et al.* 1980. Alcohol consumption and high density lipoprotein cholesterol in marathon runners. *New Engl. J. Medicine, 303:* 1159–1161.

Williams, R. S., Schocker, D. D., Morey, M. et al. 1981. Medical aspects of competitive distance running. *Postgrad. Med. 70:* 41–51.

Wood, P. D., Haskell, W. L., Blair, S. N. *et al.* 1983. Increased exercise level and plasma lipoprotein concentrations: a one year randomised controlled study in sedentary, middle-aged men. *Metabolism, 32:* 31–39.

DATA SOURCES FOR TABLES

Table 2.1 Durnin, J. G. V. A. & Passmore, R. 1967. *Energy, Work and* Leisure. Heinemann, London.

Tables 2.2; 2.3; 5.3 and 8.3. Newsholme, E. A. & Leech, A. R. 1983. *Biochemistry for the Medical Sciences,* John Wiley & Sons Ltd., London.

Table 4.1 Felig, P. & Wahren, J. 1975. Fuel homeostasis in exercise. *New Engl. J. Med. 293:* 1078–1084.

Hall, G. M. & Lucke, J. N., Masheter, K. *et al.* 1981. Metabolic and hormonal changes during prolonged exercise in the horse.
In *Biochemistry of Exercise* 1V.A. (Ed. Poortmans, J. & Niset, G.) University Park Press, Baltimore, pp. 88–92.

Paul, P., Holmes, W. L. 1975. Free fatty acids and glucose metabolism during increased energy expenditure and after training. *Medicine and Science in Sports, 7:* 176–184.

Table 5.1 Costill, D. L., Daniels, J., Evans, W. *et al.* 1976. Skeletal muscle enzymes and fibre composition in male and female track athletes. *J. Applied Physiol. 40:* 149–154.

Guy, P. S. & Snow, D. H. 1977. A preliminary survey of skeletal muscle fibre types in equine and canine species. *J. Anat. 124:* 499–500.

Snow, D. H. & Guy, P. S. 1980. Muscle fibre type composition of a number of limb muscles in different types of horse. *Res. Vet. Sci. 28:* 137–144.

Table 8.1 Hartung, G. H., Foreyt, J. P., Mitchell, R. E. *et al.* 1980. Relationship of diet to high-density-lipoprotein cholesterol in middle-aged marathon runners, joggers and inactive men. *New Engl. J. Med. 302:* 357–361.

Table 8.2 Opie, L. H. 1975. Sudden death and sport, *Lancet, i,* 263–266.

INDEX